FLORIDA UNDER SAIL

A Guide to Cruises, Beaches, Islands, and More

FLORIDA UNDER SAIL

A Guide to Cruises, Beaches,

by Janet and
Gordon Groene

illustrated by Dale Swensson

Islands, and More

Country Roads Press
CASTINE • MAINE

Published by Country Roads Press
P.O. Box 286, Lower Main Street
Castine, Maine 04421

Text and cover design by Janet Patterson.
Illustrations by Dale Swensson
Typesetting by Typeworks.

ISBN 1-56626-055-8

Library of Congress Cataloging-in-Publication Data

Groene, Janet.
    Florida under sail : a guide to cruises, beaches, islands & more /
by Janet Groene and Gordon Groene.
        p.   cm.
    Includes index.
    ISBN 1-56626-055-8 : $9.95
    1. Florida—Guidebooks.   2. Sailing—Florida—Guidebooks.
I. Groene, Gordon.   II. Title
F309.3.G75   1994
917.5904′63—dc20   94-6925
                                                        CIP

Printed in the United States of America.
10 9 8 7 6 5 4 3 2 1

To Gina Smyth and the late Peter R. Smyth,
founders of The Florida Cruising Directory

Contents

Introduction

When we arrived in Florida to move aboard the sloop that was to be our home for ten years, everything we owned was in our van, and all our hopes and dreams were tied to azure waters and billowing sails. Since then, writing assignments have taken us all over the world under power and sail, but Florida's appeal as a seaside destination has never faded for us. Welcome on board!

8,400 MILES OF SHORELINE

One of the state's tourism slogans was "Florida from coast to coast to coast," a reminder that Florida is made up of many kinds of seas and sands, coral reefs and coastal communities, remote islands and rustic riverfronts.

No other mainland state can offer such dazzling Atlantic sunrises and such golden Gulf sunsets. At Key West, you can see them both from the same anchorage.

The tireless Atlantic laps at the state's eastern shores from the Georgia border to its southern tip. The Gulf of Mexico rims its western shore. Florida Bay is formed by the crook of the Keys. The Everglades, often called a river of grass, form one of the largest and most unusual water wildernesses in the world. Florida is also home to Lake Okeechobee, the second largest body of water entirely within the United States.

Florida has 1,000 miles of beaches and 8,400 miles of shoreline. More than 4,000 known shipwrecks nestle in reefs and sands off Florida shores. Inland, the state has 7,710 natural lakes

Anchoring at Cowpens,
Plantation Yacht Harbor Light

of 10 acres or more, and 1,711 rivers and streams.

The Intracoastal Waterway can take Florida boaters all the way to Maine in protected waters. The Suwannee is one of the most famous rivers in story and song, and the St. Johns River is one of the nation's major waterways. Barges with up to 8 feet of draft can navigate the river for 150 miles. Silver Springs, famed for its glass-bottom boats, has been hosting tourists since 1896. At Crystal Springs, where fresh water boils up into the salt sea, you can snorkel with manatees.

A MARITIME TRADITION

Florida has been a maritime state since before the first Spanish and French explorers stepped ashore here in the sixteenth century. The oldest canoe ever found in the western world was dug out of the primeval ooze at DeLeon Springs. Long before Jamestown or Plymouth Rock, St. Augustine was a thriving seaside community. Even earlier, a short-lived settlement was made on the Gulf side at Pensacola.

Jonathan Dickinson, who one day would become mayor of Philadelphia, was shipwrecked in the wilds of Florida in 1696 while sailing home from Jamaica. Battling Indians, starvation, snakes, bugs, and disease, he made his way home on foot.

For centuries, Florida's only highways were her waters. As recently as the 1920s, a barefoot mailman served communities along roadless sands on what is now the Gold Coast. The Keys were not connected to the mainland until the 1930s. Until then, many of the Keys' cultural and financial ties were to the Bahamas rather than to the wilderness that was Florida.

BY LAND OR BY SEA

Our aim is to get you into, on, and near Florida's waters by any means possible—not necessarily, despite our title, only under sail. Beaches are never very far away, and you can drive right onto some of them. Lighthouses and maritime museums are found throughout the state. Aquariums, wildlife centers for seabirds and endangered manatees, and sealife research stations are a statewide passion.

Although we all like to think in terms of swashbuckling and sailing, some of the most dramatic sightseeing cruises are aboard stodgy, small, slow pontoon boats on the most quiet, narrow backwaters. These waters whirl with wildlife when you least expect it.

An alligator suddenly turns the satin surface to froth and grabs an unwary bird. A manatee sounds right next to the boat, blinks at you, and sinks quietly to resume munching water hyacinth. You're staring, mesmerized, at the wake that your boat is making when suddenly two dolphins surface and look at you with a big grin.

Take a windjammer out of Key West to view the sunset, or board a sloop out of St. Petersburg for a two-week sail to the Dry Tortugas. Sail out of the Keys on a dive boat, to scuba over living coral reefs. Fly over swamps in an airboat or a swamp buggy. There's no better way to probe the secrets of marshlands.

DON'T FORGET DISNEY

No visit to Florida would be complete without at least a day or two at Walt Disney World, which is a maritime phenomenon in itself. Although it's inland, Walt Disney World has miles of chalk-white sand beaches, man-made combers seven feet high, more boats than most navies of the world, lazy rivers, and some of the fanciest steamboats that ever carried a riverboat gambler.

Everywhere, the sense of whimsy wins over even the most humorless cynic. Dock at the Port Orleans Resort, where you'll find the Rue D'Baga. The Yacht and Beach Club Resort looks more like Cape Cod than Cape Cod does. The steel bands and straw market at the Caribbean Beach Resort transport you to the islands. And everywhere in Walt Disney World there are boats and water for fun, for transportation, or just to serve as shining scenery while you rest your tired feet.

You could spend a lifetime discovering all of Florida's seaside villages, dark and historic rivers, waterfront ghost towns, sizzling oceanfront cities, Indian shell mounds, and beaches of all lengths and widths. Come, sail Florida with us.

ABOUT HANDICAPPED ACCESS

Because of the nature of some seagoing and shoreside listings throughout this book, wheelchair access may be limited or may require advance planning. Call ahead.

FLORIDA UNDER SAIL

A Guide to Cruises, Beaches, Islands, and More

Cruising Under Sail

ABOUT CREWED SAILBOATS

Most of the windjammers that sail New England in the summertime go deep into the Caribbean for the winter, so don't expect Florida to be a southern version of Maine. If you are looking for weeklong cruises under sail in Florida, especially aboard a windjammer, you'll have to look long and hard.

The Sunshine State is popular with bareboaters (sailors who rent the boat "bare" and do all the crewing themselves), so it's more difficult for a crewed boat to make a go of it here. However, any boat rental company can arrange for a licensed captain to be put aboard the sailboat of your choice, with cook and crew too, if you like.

Many charter operators offer overnight sailing adventures with congenial and competent owner-crews. Finding the right one is a matter of finding out who's where when you want to go. Many of the saltiest boats are owned and operated by liveaboards who ran away to sea to seek their fortune. They headquarter in Fort Lauderdale this year, St. Thomas the next, and Cannes the year after that, hosting guests only as much as necessary to support themselves.

They'll know all the best and most exotic cruising grounds: the Dry Tortugas, the Marquesas, the 10,000 Islands, Pine Island Sound, the Florida Keys, and, if you want to go "overseas," the Bahamas. Many liveaboards specialize in scuba diving, shelling, or snorkeling the best reefs. Most are quintessential hosts, eager to please you and your family with the sail of a lifetime. And, because they sail all year, they can regale you for hours with sea lore. Their boats are their homes, so they maintain them meticulously, and it's a matter of pride with them to treat guests like family.

Most liveaboards can be found through ads in recent issues of *Cruising World, Sail,* or *Yachting* magazines. You might also contact charter brokers who advertise in these publications to learn what crewed boats will be in Florida when you plan to go. See the box below.

In some cases we have not included an address because the boats sail from different ports at different times. If we list only a telephone number, it is because you must call ahead for

---

WHAT TO ASK BEFORE YOU BOOK A CHARTER

Before booking, ask questions about the boat, the crew, and how long the charter has been in operation. Find out if the broker has been aboard the boat. Get the names of some previous guests, and talk to them. Learn exactly what you're expected to bring or to do. Some charters are floating resorts; on others, you must help with the sailing, cooking, and swabbing. Find out what rules or limitations exist. Some charters do not accept very young children; some do not allow smoking.

Ask what meals and drinks are provided. On some cruises you are expected to eat certain meals out or bring your own food or drinks. If you're going on a day cruise, find out whether food and beverages are included, are sold on board, or should be brought aboard. You may be required to bring provisions, or you may be prohibited from doing so.

reservations and instructions about boarding, parking, or how to find the dock.

NORTHEAST FLORIDA

Southern Wind sails out of the Conch House Marina in St. Augustine. Dennis and Jeannette Dean had this seagoing, seventy-six-foot double-ender custom made for them in California. They sailed the cutter-rigged boat down the coast, through the Panama Canal, into an encounter with pirates off Cuba, and finally to St. Augustine.

The spacious, beamy, sea-kindly boat takes small groups out by the day to see the sea, view historic St. Augustine and the fort from the water, have a buffet lunch, and sunbathe on wide decks. Below, there's a big, air-conditioned saloon. There's also a covered deck with wet bar topside for those who prefer shade to sun.

Best of all, the Deans own one of St. Augustine's loveliest old homes, where they offer bed and breakfast. Each antique-furnished room has a private bath. Take your continental breakfast in the parlor or out onto one of the

balconies. Ask about sleep-and-sail packages. 18 Cordova Street, St. Augustine. 904-825-3623.

**SOUTHWEST FLORIDA
AND THE GULF OF MEXICO**

Annapolis Sailing School offers a variety of liveaboard cruises out of the Marina Beach Resort Hotel in St. Petersburg. These cruises can be tailored to individual interests and abilities and can accommodate nonsailors, but they're aimed primarily at the person who wants to learn sailing, pilotage, seamanship, and navigation. Annapolis Sailing School, Box 3334, Annapolis, MD 21403. 800-638-9192 or 410-267-7205.

Dancing Dolphin is a forty-foot, cutter-rig sailboat offering custom charters and four-hour sunset cruises out of Myers Beach Marina, 703 Fisherman's Wharf, across from Snug Harbor in Fort Myers Beach. Call 813-463-9552 or, after 6:00 P.M., 813-463-4630.

Captain Quinn's Catamaran Tours sail daily out of Marco Island to tack among the 10,000 Islands, watching the abundant bird life and stopping at likely beaches to look for seashells. 813-642-2740.

Florida Sailing and Cruising School is primarily just that, but you're welcome to come along for the ride aboard a salty sailboat in the thirty-five- to forty-foot range. You'll spend a week or two on board with a capable captain, sailing as far as the winds allow and cruising such spots as Cayo Costa Island, Boca Grande Pass, Gasparilla Island, Sanibel, and Matanzas Pass. You can help with the sailing if you like, but your captain does all the piloting and navigation aboard the six-day Great Getaway sail or the ten-day Offshore Adventure out of Fort Myers. Southwest Florida Yachts, 3444 Marinatown Lane N.W., North Fort Myers. 800-262-7939 or 813-656-1339.

International Sailing School is a small and friendly family operation that tailors its hospitality to its guests' needs. If learning to sail is your goal, they'll take up to three students at a time on their Catalina 22. For liveaboard cruising out of Charlotte Harbor, their Catalina 30 accommodates up to four guests. You'll sail twenty to thirty miles each day, and at the end of the day you'll watch the sunset at an anchorage or dock. Shoreside

accommodations and dinners can be arranged nightly if you prefer.

The school's docks are at Burnt Store Marina and Country Club, a full resort with suites, dining, tennis, supplies, slips, car rental, and a twenty-seven-hole golf complex. International Sailing School, 3164 Matacumbe Key Road, Punta Gorda. 813-639-7492 or 800-824-5040.

Island Rover is a seventy-two-foot schooner that sails on two-hour cruises of the Gulf of Mexico twice during the day and once daily to see the sunset. Island Tall Ship Excursions is located under the Matanzas Bridge in Fort Myers Beach. 813-765-7447.

The Moorings has been specializing in sailing charters for decades and is one of the most respected names in the business. Sail away for a week or two to the company's own, secret world of scuba sites, beaches, barrier islands, rustic marinas, and fishing holes. The fleet is made up of customized Beneteau sailboats called the ***Moorings 38***, ***Moorings 432***, and ***Moorings 51***, all of them built to the Moorings' specifications for chartering in comfort. The boats are available either with captain only (you do the cooking and cleanup) or with captain and cook. Qualified sailors can also rent boats for bareboating. The Moorings Suncoast, The Harborage at Bayboro, 1110 Third Street, St. Petersburg, FL 33701. 800-368-9994 or 813-896-7900.

Sea Trader Cruises sail out of Harbour Island, Tampa, on sunset and sightseeing cruises for parties of six aboard a thirty-eight-foot sailboat. Bring your own provisions if you like, or ask the skipper to have a caterer set up lunch, cocktails, or dinner. 813-286-8512.

Sea Excursion sails out of Marco Island, taking up to six passengers out into the Gulf on two-hour sunset cruises or half-day sunshine sails to picnic islands or shelling beaches. 813-642-6400.

Sea Sense is a sailing school founded by women for women. Headquartered in New London, Connecticut, the school is based on Florida's Gulf coast during the winter. Weeklong coastal cruises run from mid-November through early May. You'll live aboard for a week while learning the ropes. Three-day sailing adventures are also available. Sea Sense, 25 Thames Street, New London, CT 06320. 203-444-1404 or 800-332-1404.

Womanship, based in Annapolis, Maryland, offers learn-to-sail cruises out of Florida ports, as well as "passage-maker" cruises (long passages such as an ocean crossing or a nonstop Maine to Florida trip) that begin or end in Florida. September through June, Womanship has bases in Southeast Florida and on the Florida Gulf coast. Groups of women, who so far have ranged in age from eighteen to seventy-five, have the adventure of a lifetime. Although Womanship's "Nobody yells" approach is a favorite with women, the company will also take families or couples. Seven-, five-, and three-day cruise courses and passage-making cruises are available in Florida and worldwide. 410 Severn Avenue, Annapolis, MD 21403. 410-269-0784 or 800-342-9295.

THE PANHANDLE (Northwest Florida)

Flying Eagle is a sixty-five-foot steel gaff-rigged tops'l schooner that sails three times a day from Harbor Cove Marina in Destin into the emerald green waters of the Gulf of Mexico. Up to thirty-nine passengers can enjoy the spacious decks.

The Flying Eagle
sails three times a day

There's a head—bathroom for you landlubbers—on board. You must bring your own refreshments, suntan lotion (no oil, please), and deck shoes or other rubber-soled footwear that won't scratch the teak decks. Harbor Cove Marina, behind A.J.'s Restaurant, one-quarter mile east of the Destin Bridge on US 98. 904-837-3700, 837-2222, or 837-4986. Reservations are preferred, but walk-ons are welcome when space allows.

Bombay Sailing Charters and **Destiny Sailing Charters** offer morning, afternoon, snorkeling, shelling, moonlight, and sunset cruises in the Gulf of Mexico and to Shell Island out of Panama City Beach. Bombay: 904-234-7794; Destiny: 904-234-7245.

SOUTHEAST FLORIDA

Coconut Grove

A visit to this tropical Eden is an essential part of any Miami visit. The marina, nestled in a lagoon and surrounded by a forest of palms, is located within walking distance of some of Florida's saltiest waterfront restaurants and best hotels, including the five-star Grand Bay, home of the world-famous Regine's nightclub.

The following boats are based here and available for charter through **Jubilee Yacht Charters**. 203-655-7227 or 800-922-4871.

Calypso Poet is a fifty-foot trimaran with four queen-size berths, three heads (including one with tub), and air-conditioning. Just tell the captain where you want to go and for how long. Bring your own provisions for the cook to prepare, or let the cook plan provisions for you.

Freedom II is a fifty-one-foot Morgan with two private cabins with heads, a spacious saloon, and a big, destroyer-style wheel that the captain will let you try. She's available with captain; you bring and prepare the food.

Dances with Waves is a forty-two-foot Catalina sloop carrying 797 square feet of canvas. Woody and glowing below, she has an owner's stateroom with head forward and twin cabins aft sharing a head with shower. The captain does the sailing unless you want to help; you plan and prepare the provisions.

FLORIDA KEYS

Annapolis Sailing School offers six-day liveaboard cruises for four people out of Marathon aboard a thirty-seven-foot O'Day sloop or a Morgan 44, each with fore and aft double cabins. Whether you take the cruise as an intense sailing course or as a sightseeing ride on which you help with the chores, this is high-seas adventure at its best. Also available are cruises to the Dry Tortugas out of the school's St. Petersburg base. 800-638-9192.

Appledore, a gaff-rigged schooner that was built and sailed around the world by Herb and Doris Smith, sails Maine in the summertime and comes to Key West for the winter. Sign on for a five-hour snorkel sail to a coral reef, a starlight champagne cruise, or the stunning sunset cruise with hors d'oeuvres, champagne, beer, wine, and soft drinks (call for reservations). The boat leaves from Land's End Marina in front of the Waterfront Market at the end of Williams Street. 305-296-9992, November to May.

Saturday's Child is an aft-cockpit, 35.5-foot sloop with two private cabins plus another double bunk in the saloon. Everyone shares one head.

You can have either a captain or a captain and cook aboard as you cruise the Keys, cross to the Bahamas, or venture out from Key West to the Marquesas and Dry Tortugas. *Saturday's Child* is booked through **Florida Yacht Charters**. She's based at the Miami Beach Marina or the Land's End Marina in Key West. The company also offers bareboats, learn-to-sail courses, and flotilla cruising in which you sail the boat, but in the company of more experienced skippers. 800-537-0050 or 305-532-8600.

Southernmost Sailing lets you choose the captain, the itinerary, and the boat from a list that includes a Hunter 34, a Morgan 36, a Gemini 32, and a couple of forty-footers. Boats are available by the day or week, and you can also arrange to sleep on board the night before sailing if you like. Shop Key West supermarkets for your own provisions. You'll also do the cooking and cleaning; the captain does the sailing, navigation, and piloting, but you're welcome to help. Southernmost Sailing, Inc., Box 369, Key West, FL 33041. 305-745-2430.

Dream Chaser is a forty-one-foot trimaran that can carry up to six people on scuba, snorkel, twilight, sunset dinner, or personalized cruises (such as its Overnight on the Reef package). Let Capt. Bob and Linda Leighton whisk you away from the crowds. Find the boat at Land's End Marina, 201 William Street, Key West, FL. 305-745-4449.

Reef Chief is a classic sixty-five-foot schooner that sails Key West waters to fish, snorkel, dive for lobster, or see the sunset. Use the captain's iced cooler, snorkel or scuba gear, and underwater camera. Head north on US 1 from Key West, right at the second traffic light on County 941. After half a mile, turn right at Vicky's Restaurant onto 4th Avenue, then go one block and turn left on Front Street to Safe Harbour Marina parking lot. 305-292-1345.

Sebago is a speedy, sprightly, state-of-the-art catamaran that sails morning and afternoon for snorkeling, then returns in the afternoon to pick up passengers for a two-hour sunset sail complete with free champagne, beer, wine, and soft drinks. She's docked at the ends of Front and William Streets. Reservations essential. 305-294-5687.

Spirit is a forty-one-foot racing sailboat that makes three trips daily to see, dive, or snorkel the living coral reefs off Key West. Ice, use of the cooler, trolling gear, and instruction are free.

Snorkel gear and an underwater camera are available. There's an added charge for scuba trips. Sign on with Capt. Cal Harris. At day's end, there's also a sunset cruise. From Key West, head north on US 1 and turn right on County 941 to Oceanside Marina. Reservations are essential. 305-296-1056.

FORT LAUDERDALE

Blue Water Yacht Charters has a fleet of catamarans and monohulls ranging from an Endeavourcat 30 to a Solaris 42, a Hardin 45, and a Morgan Out Island 41. The boats sleep six to ten people and are available with a captain or an American Sailing Association captain-instructor. Cruise the Keys or Bahamas, or take the advanced cruising course, which takes five to six weeks, and sail across the Atlantic. The next step after that, say instructors, is to sail around the world in your own boat! Blue Water Yacht Charters, 1414 South Andrews Avenue, Fort Lauderdale, FL 33316. 305-768-0846 or 800-522-2992.

ABOUT SAILING SCHOOLS

We list sailing schools—many of which also offer powerboat courses—in this book because most of them offer low-key, liveaboard, captained cruising for people who want a sailing vacation along with high-energy sailing courses. While you won't be responsible for the sailing and piloting, these are usually working vacations in which everyone pitches in to swab the decks, cook meals, make up bunks, and wash dishes.

Most of these boats carry no more than six "students." If you want a cruise more than a course, it's best to book the entire boat and tell the skipper that you want to sail and sightsee more than take sunsights and fine-tune the jib.

Write to several schools to find one that meets your goals. Some are for women only. Some offer ASA certification, which qualifies you to captain your own bareboat next time around. Some emphasize racing; others cruising. The **Chapman School of Seamanship** offers a wide range of courses from small boat sailing to professional mariner training, boat surveying, and marine electronics. 4343 S.E. St. Lucie Blvd., Stuart 34997, 800-225-2841 or 407-283-8130.

INSIDER TIP

When booking a liveaboard cruise, always ask if **shoreside accommodations** are available as an add-on to the package. Often, highly discounted rates are available at or near the marina for the nights before or after your cruise.

Cruising Under Power

SIGHTSEEING AND DINNER CRUISES

It may come as a surprise to you that the most common Florida passenger boats by far are not windjammers but replica Mississippi riverboat–style paddle wheelers. These boats offer sightseeing, dining, dancing, moonlight, and sunset cruises, often with a wedding party or two aboard to add to the festive atmosphere.

Galleons and sailing ships brought the first conquerors to Florida, but it was sternwheel and sidewheel steamboats that pioneered Florida tourism. Today's boats simply relive the days when riverboats left Charleston on a regular schedule, to steam up the St. Johns River. They brought winter-weary passengers in search of sunshine; they returned loaded with crates of oranges.

During the Civil War, steamboats served the state by carrying personnel and goods. It was in Florida that the battleship *Maine* took on coal for her trip to Havana Harbor, where she was blown up and became the most important symbol of the Spanish-American War. Diesel power has replaced steam, and most of the paddle wheels today are phonies, but the state's timeless waters flow on, unchanged.

Second in popularity to steamboats are

pontoon boats, plain and practical but beamy with very shallow draft. They seat passengers for excursions deep into small lakes and rivers where keel boats cannot reach.

In terms of boat ownership, Florida is fourth in the nation, behind California, Michigan, and Minnesota, but in terms of megayachts, brutish sportfishermen, and transient sailboats in their restless routes around the world, Florida is first. To take one of the cruises listed below is to be a part of this exciting seagoing scene.

In many cases we haven't given home port addresses for these cruises. It's essential to **call first**, make reservations, and learn exactly where to find the boat when you will be boarding it.

SOUTHWEST FLORIDA

The **Admiral Dinner Boat** is a 400-passenger triple-decker that offers dinner, sightseeing, luncheon, and dinner-dance cruises. The boat sails out of Clearwater Beach Marina. 813-462-2628 or 800-444-4814.

Aboard a fast, thirty-foot **Aqua Adventures** cutter you'll speed to the most interesting reefs and wrecks off Marco Island to snorkel, sightsee, or scuba dive. Wetsuits, snorkel equipment, and dive gear (for qualified divers) are available for rent. The boat sails out of Factory Bay Marina. 813-394-DIVE.

Captain Anderson, a three-decker, was a Florida fixture for generations. Now it's been replaced by the sleek, elegant **Lady Anderson**. She cruises out of St. Petersburg in winter, featuring bird feeding and dolphin watch cruises Tuesday through Friday (in summer, you'll find the *Lady Anderson* in Panama City Beach). Dining and dancing cruises sail in the moonlight; scenic luncheon cruises also sail from the beach causeway. Also popular are the **Gospel Music Cruises** starring southern Gospel groups that raise the roof with clapping and song. Reservations are essential. 813-367-7804.

Captain Nemo's Pirate Ship makes two-hour raids on the Gulf of Mexico three times daily. Refreshments are included in the fare. No sailings on Sundays. Home port is Clearwater Beach Marina. 813-446-2587.

The Cortez Fleet offers bird feeding/dolphin watch cruises aboard a beamy, shoal-draft cruiser with two big, open decks. Capt. Jim and Barbara

Berry will take you sightseeing around Anna Maria Island or on a beachcombing trip to historic Egmont Key, site of Fort Dade, which is slowly being reclaimed by nature. Here, on an island that can't be reached by road, you can swim, snorkel, and collect seashells. The Cortez docks are on the east side of the bridge on State 684 west of Bradenton. 813-794-1223.

Crazy Clam sails daily from Marco Island to the 10,000 Islands for sightseeing, shelling, and snorkeling. By night, she does dinner cruises with dancing and entertainment. 813-642-0061.

Curveball, John and Pam Stops's thirty-six-foot catamaran hull powerboat, cruises out of Marco Island or the Isles of Capri. On sightseeing cruises, you're likely to see manatees and porpoises among the 10,000 Islands. On shelling cruises, Captain Stops chooses a secluded beach where you're likely to gather hatfuls of whelks, scallop shells, conch shells, tellins, cone shells, and much more. Or take the sunset cruise to chase the sun into the Gulf of Mexico. 813-394-8000.

Everglades Jungle Cruises offers a three-hour narrated cruise up the Caloosahatchee River out of Fort Myers. Along the riverbanks you'll see native orchids, wading birds, alligators, and worlds of plant and animal life typical of a subtropical river basin. Also offered are dining and entertainment cruises. Boats dock at the City Yacht Basin at the end of Lee Street in Fort Myers. 813-334-7474.

Florida Sailing and Cruising School is primarily just that, but you're welcome to come along for the ride aboard a salty Grand Banks classic trawler. You'll live on board for a week or two, cruising such spots as Cayo Costa Island, Boca Grande Pass, Gasparilla Island, Sanibel, and Matanzas Pass. Meals are included. Southwest Florida Yachts, 3444 Marinatown Lane N.W., North Fort Myers. 800-262-7939 or 813-656-1339.

Try a **FunKruz** aboard the *Europa* out of St. Petersburg or Fort Myers for five or six hours of daytime dining and sightseeing or a starlight cruise with dining and dancing. Las Vegas–style entertainment and casino-style gambling add to the fun. 813-393-5110 .

Island Princess wends a fourteen-mile route through the 10,000 Islands south of Marco Island. The two-hour cruises, which can carry up to forty-nine people, sail twice a day. Nature sightings include mangrove communities, wading birds,

birds of prey, and dolphins. The boat sails from the Port of the Islands, east of Marco Island on Tamiami Trail. 813-394-3101.

Snorkel cruises, for the purpose of collecting a sackful of succulent, pearly white scallops, are offered by Capt. Robbie Edge. You'll need snorkel gear plus a sack and a Florida freshwater fishing license. Homosassa River Retreat, 10605 Halls Drive Road, Homosassa Springs. 904-628-7072.

Lady Chadwick sails the sea green, sparkling waters of Pine Island Sound to faraway islands for lunch. Choose to land at rustic Cabbage Key, once the domain of mystery novelist Mary Roberts Rinehart, or continue to exclusive Useppa Island, named for a pirate's captive, the beautiful Joseffa. Either way, you'll have a two-hour shore leave to eat, then stroll around your choice of the tiny, historic islands and learn their secrets. The *Lady Chadwick* also serves a continental breakfast cruise and a sunset nature cruise. Dolphin sightings are almost guaranteed; the close-ups of osprey and snakebirds, which nest in the navigation markers that pass just under your nose, are a shutterbug's delight.

On Saturday nights, take the lavish buffet cruise at day's end. Schedules and themes vary, so call ahead for information and reservations. Getting there is half the fun; the ship sails out of colorful South Seas Plantation Yacht Harbour on Captiva Island, which is a long, scenic drive from the mainland via beautiful Sanibel Island, which lies off Fort Myers. 813-472-5300.

Le Barge sails daily except Monday from Marina Jack in Sarasota on two-hour cruises among the mangrove islands to view the rookeries and bird sanctuaries. Evening cruises have entertainment. The galley is open if you want to order food. 813-366-6116.

Marina Jack II, a 100-foot replica Mississippi riverboat, sails the calm waters of Sarasota Bay while you dine in air-conditioned (or heated) comfort. After-dark cruises have entertainers. Schedules vary, so call for information and reservations. 813-366-9255.

Miss Barnegat Light cruises to the Dry Tortugas. The ninety-foot, high-speed catamaran leaves on Friday evening for the 125-mile overnight sail to the islands, and returns Sunday afternoon. The living is sporty and relaxed, suitable for singles, couples, or families.

Bring your own sleeping bag and be

prepared to bed down in a bunk until 4:00 to 5:00 A.M., when twenty-four hours of fishing begins. The destination is the Florida Straits, famed for supersize pompano, snapper, mackerel, and cobia. You'll have a good view of historic Fort Jefferson and endless entertainment from seabirds, dancing dolphins, and flying fish. Keep in mind that most of your fellow passengers will be serious meat fishermen who are intent on the catch. Meals are hearty, hot-water showers abundant, and the camaraderie great, but a cruise liner it isn't.

The *Miss Barnegat Light* is found under the south end of the Sky Bridge on Fort Myers Beach, next to Gulf Star Marina at Old Bonita Fish Docks. 813-463-5665 or 765-0382.

Seafood Shack Showboat relives the days of fancy ladies and riverboat gamblers while cruising along Anna Maria Island and Longboat Key in the protected waters of the Intracoastal Waterway. Aboard are two lounges; the lower deck is enclosed and air-conditioned. 813-794-3766.

Show Queen is a 150-passenger triple-decker that sails out of Clearwater Beach Marina to get a good view of the beaches, city skyline, and the Gulf. Dinner, sightseeing, and morning and sunset cruises are scheduled. 813-461-3113.

Sunshine Tours. Aboard the party boats *Sunshine Express* (12 passengers), *Miss Sunshine* (40 passengers), or *Double Sunshine* (125-passengers), take a shelling excursion, sunset or sightseeing cruises, or a lunch cruise on the Marco River to the end-of-the-world fishing village of Goodland. The boats are based at the Marco Island Marina. 813-642-4515.

Scurvy Dog is Capt. George Dailey's swift and sleek thirty-eight-foot Bertram. He'll take you out by the half day, day, or overnight from the Marco River Marina. Cruise the Gulf in air-conditioned comfort with cellular phone, full bath, and all the sophisticated electronics of a seagoing yacht. 813-642-9639.

Starlite Princess has a paddle wheel, all the gingerbread grillwork of a Mississippi riverboat, and leisurely dining while you watch the waves go by. Reservations are essential. She sails out of 401 Second Street East, Indian Rocks Beach. 813-595-1212 or 800-722-6645.

THE RIVER OF MANY NAMES

Look at a Florida map, and you'll see that ribbons of water run between the mainland and such eastern barrier islands as Jacksonville Beach, Anastasia Island off St. Augustine, Merritt Island, and Palm Beach. Although they're called by such names as the Banana River, the Indian River, the Halifax, Tolomato, and Matanzas, most of them are not rivers but brackish tidal waters. Forming the Intracoastal Waterway, which can take boaters down the entire east coast of the state in protected water, these "rivers" are well traveled by local sightseeing boats. (The Gulf Coast also has a protected Intracoastal Waterway.) If you take one cruise in each major community, you'll end up seeing almost every inch of the eastern ICW. **Call ahead for information and to make reservations.**

Because these waterways face each area's most elegant homes, most significant historic sites, and/or barrier islands rich in natural history, they form some of Florida's most rewarding, all-weather cruising grounds.

Gatsby's Little River Queen is a gingerbread-decorated paddle wheeler that cruises the Banana River out of Cocoa Beach through the 1,000-acre Merritt Island Wildlife Refuge, which is home to 310 species of birds, 25 species of mammals, and 65 species of amphibians and reptiles. Sightseeing, lunch, dinner, and Dixieland cruises are available. 407-783-2380.

Island Princess is a private, 155-passenger excursion boat for Indian River Plantation, a Mobil Four-Star, AAA Four-Diamond resort on Hutchinson Island. Packages at the 326-unit resort include sightseeing, sunset cruises, and other sails aboard the boat, as well as golf, tennis, a children's program, and other amenities of a first-class resort. Indian River Plantation is located on State A1A in Stuart. 800-444-3389 or 407-225-6990.

Manatee Queen sails the Jupiter Island–Loxahatchee River area in a choice of sunset cruises, historical lectures, and nature itineraries. The boat docks at Charley's Crab, 1000 US l, Jupiter. 407-744-2191.

Ramblin' Rose, a Mississippi-style riverboat, cruises the Intracoastal Waterway out of Delray Beach among the millionaire mansions of Manalpan north or Boca Raton south. Dining, sightseeing, and dancing cruises sweep you back to the days of gamblin' men and fancy ladies in air-conditioned comfort. 407-243-0686.

Sea Pirate is a double-decker power yacht that cruises out of Melbourne to look for dolphins, picnic on a windswept island, and sightsee along the Intracoastal Waterway. If you're lucky enough to be on board during a space launch, you'll have a front-row seat. Take an afternoon dolphin watch cruise or a buffet dinner cruise at sunset to watch for dolphins at play in the dying sun. Reservations are essential. Shooter's Dock in Melbourne. 407-724-0024.

Spirit of St. Joseph has a bright red sternwheel, three decks, and an itinerary along the Intracoastal Waterway around Fort Pierce. Sightseeing, dining, and entertainment cruises are available. The boat docks behind the St. Lucie County Historical Museum. 800-344-TGIF or 407-467-BOAT.

Star of Palm Beach is a replica paddle wheeler that offers sightseeing and dining cruises through the backyards of some of the nation's richest and most powerful families in Palm Beach. The ship sails from Singer Island. 407-842-0882.

Tiny Cruise Line is the right name for this delightful little character boat and the intimate, low-key cruises she supplies out of Daytona Beach. Early photographs show a fantail launch much like this one that carried hotel guests on river cruises at the turn of the century.

Capt. Jim Lindner and his wife Kathy had the boat built to order, with an outboard motor secreted under a varnished hatch that looks as though it hides an 1890s steam engine. Taking people on cruises is the Lindners' life, and they treat folks like family.

Along the waterways, including the Halifax River and also shallow waters where other boats can't venture, you'll see old downtown Daytona Beach with its Art Deco facades. At the same time, you'll observe osprey fishing in the Halifax, leaping mullet, and playful dolphins. Along the other shore, you'll see waterfront estates, including a Victorian mansion where novelist Stephen Crane wrote *The Open Boat.* The Lindners host sightseeing, sunset, and bring-your-own picnic cruises daily except Mondays out of the Show Dock at the City Marina. 904-226-2343.

Sternwheel is a project of yachtsmen Dennis and Jeannette Dean, who were determined to offer their guests the best in hospitality aboard a truly historic craft in historic St. Augustine.

The boat, which leaves from the City Docks, downtown St. Augustine, offers lunch and dining cruises in waters around America's oldest city. Ask about packages that include bed and breakfast at the Deans' antique-furnished Southern Wind at 18 Cordova Street in St. Augustine. 904-825-3623.

Victory II and *Victory III* are shoal-draft, easy-riding excursion boats built in St. Augustine by a family that has been taking people sightseeing for generations. Although there's some narration, much of the ride is a quiet whooshing through waters that were discovered by the French in the 1500s and commanded by the Spanish until well into the nineteenth century.

No matter how much other sightseeing you do in America's oldest city, don't miss a chance to see it from the water, especially the imposing fortress **Castillo de San Marcos**, constructed 1672–1695, and the 208-foot-high stainless-steel cross that marks the place where the first Spanish explorers claimed Florida for Spain. The *Victory* boats sail daily except for Christmas on several seventy-five-minute cruises each day out of the Municipal Yacht Pier, Avenida Menendez. 904-824-1806.

THE ST. JOHNS RIVER

Miami was still a remote outpost in the 1850s when early Florida tourists streamed into the state aboard steam-driven paddle wheelers. Ships left Charleston three times a week to churn up the St. Johns River as far as Mellonville, now called Sanford. On the return trip, decks were piled high with crates of oranges. When steam ran low, crewmen went ashore to chop more wood. When a boat ran aground, they cut huge trees, built a temporary dam to raise the water level, and floated the boat free.

The coming of railroads and highways changed tourism patterns so completely that many of the once-thriving settlements along the St. Johns are ghost towns today. Still others are sleepy villages, unknown to tourists who speed by on their way to Walt Disney World. Yet the St. Johns is one of the state's most beautiful and unspoiled cruising destinations, as well as one of the best fisheries in the Southeast.

At its northern end in Jacksonville, which it splits in two, the St. Johns River is deep and wide. At Mayport, a major navy base, free ship tours are offered every weekend.

In downtown Jax, the river is aboil with private boats and commercial traffic. Water taxies whisk passengers from one side of the river to the other to hotels, restaurants, museums, and other destinations. Upstream, the river narrows in some places to dark, jungle-lined corridors. In others, it widens into vast lakes.

In the narrow stretches of the St. Johns, cruising boats wind through miles of tangled forests that are alive with wildlife, including wild monkeys that escaped during the filming of early Tarzan movies at Silver Springs. Manatees, which migrate up the river in cold weather, can be seen munching placidly among the water hyacinths. At Orange City, where **Blue Spring State Park** is one of the state's best manatee refuges, February is prime time for viewing the huge, endangered mammal.

THE ST. JOHNS, JACKSONVILLE

LA Cruise is a casual, kickback cruise out of Mayport into the open Atlantic. You can play in the casino, dine, dance to live bands, soak in one of the hot tubs, or just sit on deck and read. Take State A1A east from Jacksonville and take Ocean Street toward the navy base. Cruises are Sunday from 1:00 to 6:00 P.M., Wednesday and Saturday from 11:00 A.M. to 4:00 P.M., and Tuesday through Saturday from 7:00 P.M. to midnight. Reservations are essential. 800-752-1778

Jacksonville Water Taxis operate among the Landing, Riverwalk, the Gulf Life building, and the Chart House Restaurant. They're an economical, quick, and fun way to get from one action-packed bank of the St. Johns River to the other. Hours: Taxis operate, weather permitting, Monday through Thursday from 11:00 A.M. to 11:00 P.M., Friday and Saturday until 1:00 A.M., and Sunday until 6:00 P.M. Jacksonville's water taxis include Bass Marine 904-398-2628; Compass Rose, 904-396-0384; PJ's, 904-448-9874; St. Johns Water Taxi, 904-783-0875; and La Dolce Vita Gondola, 904-642-6357.

Viking Sun sails daily on sightseeing and dining cruises, with musical entertainment and a guide to point out the sights. On weekends, the ship cruises to Brunswick, Georgia, St. Augustine, or upstream to the old river town of Palatka. 904-398-0797.

Also offering sightseeing and dining cruises

on the St. Johns River is the ***First Lady of Jacksonville***. 904-398-0797.

Annabel Lee is a colorful paddle wheeler that churns her sightseeing way up and down the St. Johns, with magnificent views of the Jacksonville skyline. Call for schedules of sightseeing, dining and dance cruises, and instructions on parking and boarding. 904-396-2333.

Riverwalk Cruise Lines offers lunch, sightseeing, and dinner cruises, but times and prices vary, so call for reservations and schedules. Boats sail from the north bank behind the courthouse. 904-398-0797.

ST. JOHNS UPRIVER (DeLand, Sanford)

For more than a decade **Rivership *Grand Romance***, a family-run cruise line, has been introducing Orlando visitors to a part of Florida they never knew existed. Cruises depart from Sanford, an old river town, and wind north (downstream) past fields of grazing cattle, jungle foliage, reedy shorelines lined with leggy waterfowl, and markers topped by osprey nests.

Three-hour cruises include a lunch or brunch; showtime cruises include dinner and a fast-paced revue; moonlight cruises are for dinner and dancing. Also offered is an all-day cruise that travels fifty miles upstream to an ancient Indian landmark, Crow's Bluff. A two-day river cruise spends the night in the historic river town of Palatka, ninety miles downstream. In a three-night voyage, the *Grand Romance* leaves the St. Johns at Jacksonville and turns south to see the nation's oldest city, St. Augustine.

Speaking of romance, marriages can be performed aboard by the captain, who presides over about fifty ceremonies each year. Ask for details; the proprietors are very helpful with all arrangements, but advance planning is required. Rivership *Grand Romance* is based on Lake Monroe in Sanford. 407-321-5091, 800-423-7401 in Florida, or 800-225-7999 in the United States and Canada.

Airboat rides give visitors the big picture of the mighty St. Johns River, which is fed by such powerful flows as Blue Springs, DeLeon Springs, and Silver Springs. The river's origins are so humble that nobody is quite sure where it begins. A trickle here, a seepage and a swamp there,

Take a paddle wheeler downstream to a part of Florida
you never knew existed

form marshy headwaters that are too shallow to boat and too wet to walk. Airboats, which have shallow, flat-bottom hulls and are driven by airplane motors, skim over water, marsh, and dry land at heady speeds, giving passengers the wildest ride of their lives. The wildlife show is spectacular as alligators waddle out of the way and great flocks of birds flush out of the shallows. Half-hour-long airboat tours are offered daily by Lone Cabbage Fish Camp, State 520 at the St. Johns River, Cocoa. 407-632-4199.

FORT LAUDERDALE'S NEW RIVER

Today it's lined with mansions of the rich and famous, but the dark waters of the New River still whisper with history. Fort Lauderdale founder Frank Stanahan came here early in the twentieth century to trade with the Indians, and his wife became a teacher to the Seminoles. With progress came debts, speculation, and the Great Depression. Financially ruined, Stranahan chose to end his life by jumping into these waters. The Stranahan home on the river is open for tours.

Carrie B leaves from Fort Lauderdale's scenic Riverwalk for one-and-a-half-hour tours of the river, the Intracoastal Waterway, and into Port Everglades with its fleets of cruise ships, naval vessels, and millionaire yachts. Snacks and drinks are available on board. Sit outdoors on the top deck or in the air-conditioned second deck, enjoying the view through high, wide windows. S.E. 5th Avenue, Riverwalk. 305-768-9920.

The Jungle Queen has been a Fort Lauderdale classic for fifty years, and she still offers a surprisingly natural cruise through the back door of a crowded, ultramodern city. Thick jungle growth lines the river, which takes you far inland to get a glimpse of the old Florida. Sightseeing, dining, and show cruises sail daily. 801 Seabreeze Boulevard (State A1A), 305-566-5533.

The Paddlewheel Queen, a floating blues club, takes up to 300 passengers on a good-time cruise through the Venice of America while they browse the buffet, play blackjack bingo, and listen to good jazz. 2950 N.E. 32nd Avenue, Fort Lauderdale. 305-564-7659.

Water Taxi of Fort Lauderdale serves as your designated driver when you go bar hopping and restaurant roaming on Fort Lauderdale's 175 miles of waterways. You can reach many of the city's hotels, shops, and sightseeing attractions, including the Broward Center for the Performing Arts, quickly and pleasantly by water. One-way rates and day and weekly passes are sold. 305-565-5507.

BISCAYNE BAY

Nikko Gold Coast Cruises focuses on the glittering lifestyle of Miami. You'll cruise past the homes of millionaires, Bayside Marketplace with its chic shops and restaurants, marinas bristling with yachts worth millions, and historic Villa Viscaya, an Italian Renaissance mansion built in 1916. Call for schedules, reservations, and boarding information. 305-945-5461. Also see **Biscayne Bay National Underwater Park**.

THE FLORIDA KEYS (also see Chapter 4)

Admiral Busby is a big, speedy powerboat that makes two four-hour trips daily out of Key West. The *Admiral* offers scuba (including certification training), snorkeling, and underwater photography. It's found at the South Beach Motel, 508 South Street, Key West. Call 305-294-0011 between 7:00 A.M. and 11:00 P.M.

Atlantic X, registered in St. Vincent and the Grenadines, offers Las Vegas–style fun and gaming complete with casino, forty slots, dining, dancing, and live music. She sails daily out of downtown Key West at the ends of Greene and Elizabeth Streets. Reservations are essential. 305-292-1777.

Glass-bottom boat trips and sunset cruises leave daily from Hawk's Cay Resort and Marina, MM 61, Duck Key. 305-743-7000.

Glass-bottom boat undersea tours leave daily in Key West. The hull of *Discovery* has been fitted with a unique underwater viewing room that lets you watch in comfort as the sea bottom, with all its natural treasures, floats by. Margaret Street, Key West. 305-293-0099.

M/V *Holiday Cat* departs daily from the Holiday Inn Beachside in Key West to snorkel, scuba, or sightsee among the dolphins and flying fish. Aboard the sightseeing cruise to the "back" side of Key West, you thread through mangrove islands. At sunset, you can take the champagne

CRUISING WALT DISNEY WORLD

If the navies of the world were ranked according to the number of ships they have, Walt Disney World near Orlando would be the eighth largest in the world. WDW, which sprawls for miles across central Florida, has been shaped and manicured into lagoons and lakes, creeks and waterways. Splash Mountain alone has a 950,000-gallon reservoir with a flow capacity of 28,000 gallons per minute. There is no end to the skill, research, craftsmanship, and imagination that go into creating authentic replica boats and ships. Here are some of WDW's saltiest cruises:

MAGIC KINGDOM CRUISES

It's a Small World. Children adore it, and adults can't stop humming the delightful little melody that plays as you cruise through a friendly wonderland of dolls in native costume.

Jungle Cruise. In a boat that looks for all the world like the *African Queen*, you'll explore the Nile valley, an Amazon rain forest, a Southeast Asian jungle, and the African veldt for a good look at animated gorillas, elephants, and tropical birds.

Pirates of the Caribbean. The pirates almost succeed in capturing you as your treasure ship sails the Spanish Main.

Rivers of America. This bright, brassy steam paddle wheeler circles Tom Sawyer's Island, passes the Thunder Mountain Railroad, and heads into Indian Country. If you want to take a side trip to island caves and the treehouse, hop aboard a log raft. Also cruising the "river" is *Davy Crockett's Keel Boat.*

Splash Mountain. In this thrill ride, your log raft zooms down a six-story waterfall in the land of Brer Rabbit and Brer Fox. It's the longest flume chute in the world.

20,000 Leagues Under the Sea. Sail through underwater gardens aboard Captain Nemo's *Nautilus*, and find the lost city of Atlantis.

EPCOT CENTER CRUISES

Listen to the Land. This cruise takes you on a journey past different agricultural environments and into a greenhouse filled with unusual crops and examples of growing methods.

Living Seas. For information on this huge aquarium, see Chapter 3.

CRUISING WALT DISNEY WORLD (continued)

Mexico. A placid boat trip through this pavilion shows pre-Columbian, Spanish-Colonial, and modern Mexican figures, including Acapulco cliff divers.

Norway. This boat ride is splashy and exciting. You'll board a wooden Viking ship to sail past villages and ancient petroglyphs, trolls, and waterfalls before being caught in the Maelstrom.

WALT DISNEY WORLD TRANSPORTATION

Transportation, much of it by boat, is provided throughout WDW. Once your car is parked in a theme park parking lot or at a WDW hotel, you'll have a wide choice of ways to get around, including sparkling, placid waterways. Floatboats serve Disney Village Marketplace and Pleasure Island. Boats transport guests from the Yacht and Beach Club Resort, the Walt Disney Swan, and the Walt Disney Dolphin to the Disney–MGM Studios Theme Park. The Sassagoula Steamship Company takes guests of Disney's Dixie Landings Resort to Port Orleans or to Pleasure Island.

Take a shortcut across the World Showcase Lagoon in Epcot Center aboard an old-fashioned excursion boat. You can also cross Seven Seas Lagoon and Bay Lake in the Magic Kingdom by boat. All boat trips are included in WDW's one-price admission fee.

Empress Lily is permanently moored at the edge of the Buena Vista Lagoon, but she's so authentic a stern wheeler and so elegant a dining experience that a meal here is a must for the traveler who is cruising Florida. Gingerbread trim, brasses and brightwork, a wheelhouse, tall stacks, and hog chains (which were used to keep original riverboats from getting hogbacked) are all in meticulous condition. The gold leaf trim alone cost $8,000 when the ship was built in 1977.

Aboard the ship are three restaurants: the Fisherman's Deck for seafood, Steerman's Quarters for beef, and the Empress Room for gourmet dining in the Very Expensive range. Dixieland jazz in the lounge is just right for the setting. Reservations must be made well in advance. 407-828-3900.

cruise. The mailing address is Beachside Watersports and Holiday Divers, Box 2582, Key West, FL 33045. Sailing from the Holiday Inn, 3841 Roosevelt Boulevard, Key West. 800-468-4242 or 305-294-5934.

Sea-Clusive Charters sends you away on liveaboard cruises in the waters around Key West and the Marquesas. Aboard the fifty-foot motor yacht *Playmate* you'll bask in the luxuries of air-conditioning, TV, VCR, and fine cuisine. Dive reefs and wrecks, take a tour of towering Fort Jefferson, and film it all with one of *Playmate*'s underwater video cameras. Or let the crew film your dive and go home with a tape that captures it all. Only ten can be accommodated for living aboard; day charters can take up to forty folks. The mailing address is Box 431961, Big Pine Key, FL 33043. 305-872-3940.

For information on all of the following, contact the Lower Keys Chamber of Commerce. 800-872-3722 or 305-872-2411.

Captain John Sahagian's Fun Yet Charters offers ecology tours above and below the water.

Captain Buddy's Family Fun Trips

provides everything—including gear, food, drinks, and an underwater camera—to take you and your family on an island picnic, snorkeling over coral reefs, and cruising in a glass-bottom boat through the Keys' most interesting underwater scenery.

Underseas Inc. takes groups diving and snorkeling on the reefs of the marine sanctuary off the Keys. Water taxis in Southeast Florida include Key West Water Taxi, 305-745-4569, and Northern Palm Beach County Water Taxi, 407-775-2628.

NORTHWEST FLORIDA

Captain Davis Queen Fleet out of Panama City offers a dolphin feeding cruise aboard a spacious, glass-bottom party boat, the *Florida Queen*. Cruises leave nightly between 5:15 and 6:30, returning in time for your dinner reservations at the captain's Dockside Restaurant. 5550 North Lagoon Drive and Thomas Drive, Panama City Beach. 904-234-3435.

Lady Anderson spends her summers in Panama City Beach and her winters in St. Petersburg. Board this roomy new luxury boat for dinner, dancing, dining, a Gospel concert, a picnic, or sightseeing cruises on the Gulf of Mexico. 5550 North Lagoon Drive and Thomas Drive, Panama City Beach. 904-234-3435.

M/V *Stardancer* sails out of Panama City Beach to the waters of St. Andrews Bay and into the Gulf of Mexico on six-hour outings that give you plenty of time to dine, sun on three decks, dance, try the lounges, see a show, and play the casino. Like cruise liners, *Stardancer* has a cruise director to lead bingo and other shipboard activities. Panama City Beach. 800-355-7447 or 904-233-6500.

THE WINTER PARK CHAIN OF LAKES

Once a sleepy, separate winter spa for wealthy northerners who came by train, Winter Park has been swallowed by the giant amoeba that is Orlando-land, but that doesn't diminish its green and aloof charm. It's the home of Rollins College, founded in 1885. The **Morse Museum of Art** here houses one of the largest Tiffany collections in the world, and the seashell collection in the **Beal-Maltbie Museum** is one of the state's best.

Early in its development, the hamlet's lakes were connected by canals, now the setting for one of Florida's most unique powerboat cruises. In a one-hour cruise on sparkling lakes and through canals that are mere tunnels through dense woods, you'll see some of the state's most stunning old mansions, the Rollins campus, and other points of interest. The lakes and marshes abound in wildlife, but even more impressive are the trees and plants, lush and green, that embrace the boats as they squeeze under the mossy bridges and along ancient canals.

Boats leave from 10:00 A.M. to 4:00 P.M. from the eastern foot of Morse Boulevard on Lake Osceola in Winter Park. 407-644-4056. Boats and Beignets, a cruise that is followed by beignets at the chic Park Plaza Gardens, leaves Fridays at 7:00 P.M.; same telephone. Reservations are required.

THE LOVE BOAT CONNECTION

With four major cruise-ship ports, Florida is the cruise capital of the world. So exciting is the cruise scene that watching is almost as much fun

*The cruise scene is so exciting that watching
is almost as much fun as sailing*

as sailing. Cars line up along the Rickenbacker Causeway in Miami to ogle the sailing leviathans in home port—half a dozen at a time—as they fill up with thousands of happy, seabound passengers.

Helicopters spin overhead, filming the arrival of a ship carrying a famous passenger. Banner-towing planes drift back and forth, carrying such signs as "Happy Honeymoon to Jen and Marc" or "Happy 50th Birthday to Michael J."

On special occasions, entire yacht clubs turn out, fully dressed with flags fluttering, to escort a cruise liner in or out of port. During inaugural cruises, the fire department comes too, spraying huge volleys of colored water into the air.

On deck, passengers drink champagne and dodge confetti. On the dock, florists' vans jockey for position among trucks laden with pounds of beluga caviar, tons of meat and eggs, carloads of flour, and countless cases of wine. By day the dock has a festival air, and by night it's a fairyland of lightbulbs up and down masts and all over the rigging.

We've listed just some of our picks among Florida's regular cruise ships. Many other ships call here irregularly as they roam the world, and we haven't listed those. The best way to book any of these cruises is through a travel agent. The most comprehensive and authoritative guidebook to the cruise liners of the world is Ethel Blum's *The Total Traveler by Ship* (Graphic Arts Center Publishing Company, Box 10306, Portland, OR 97210).

Note that many of the cruises listed here are for one day only, and do not include a cabin. We have listed them with the "love boats" because they are big, oceangoing liners, not the smaller vessels featured elsewhere in this book. Swift and able, they give you a taste of the salt sea, out of sight of land, even if your schedule or pocketbook don't allow you to sign on for a real cruise.

Many passengers take day cruises solely for the gambling; casinos open as soon as ships are in international waters. Other day-cruise passengers want to try cruising for a day before they commit to a longer, more expensive cruise. Passage on these one-day outings starts at less than $40 per person.

A good, multiday cruise in the moderate price range runs $200 to $300 per day per person. Aboard grand luxe-class liners, rates can run as high as $1,000 per person per day. Because all activities, entertainment, children's programs, meals, and much more are included, many cruisers find they spend less on these holidays than at a resort where activities are priced separately.

For more information or to make reservations, see your travel agent.

FROM MIAMI

Three million passengers each year sail from the Port of Miami to destinations all over the world. Ships of ten major cruise lines are based here all year, including five of the largest ocean vessels in the world, each carrying more than 2,000 passengers.

American Family Cruises calls the *American Adventure* and the *American Pioneer* KinShips because they are designed for children and parents cruising together. Built originally for the Costa Line, the ships have been completely refurbished to accommodate family groups.

Carnival Cruise Lines is best known for its celebration atmosphere and moderate rates. Sailings include the 1,896-passenger *Celebration* to the Caribbean; the 2,594-passenger *Ecstasy* to

Mexico and Grand Cayman; the 2,634-passenger *Fantasy* to Nassau and Freeport; and the 1,452-passenger *Holiday* leaving every Saturday for the Yucatan and Grand Cayman.

CostaRomantica, known for its Italian style and impeccable service, sails every Sunday for the Caribbean, with alternating itineraries to the eastern and western islands.

Dolphin IV is a 588-passenger, budget-class ship that makes three- and four-day cruises to the Bahamas. The line also owns *SeaBreeze*, which carries 840 people on weeklong cruises to the Yucatan or the Bahamas.

Royal Caribbean Cruise Line's truly majestic, 2,354-berth *Majesty of the Seas* sails Sundays for the Yucatan, Grand Cayman, Ocho Rios, and a private island. Tariffs are in the high-moderate range. *Nordic Princess* takes 1,600 passengers on three- and four-day cruises to the Bahamas. *Sovereign of the Seas* carries 2,276 pampered passengers on voyages to the Bahamas, Virgin Islands, and Puerto Rico.

Tropic Star's Starlite Cruises leave daily except Saturday on day-long cruises to the Bahamas and back. On Saturday, the Cruise to Nowhere leaves at 10:00 A.M. and returns at 4:00 P.M.

FROM FORT LAUDERDALE (Port Everglades)

Discovery I has a varied schedule of affordable day cruises, some with a stop at Freeport, Grand Bahama, and others to sea and back.

Royal Viking Sun sails out of Fort Lauderdale on a Gulf of Mexico itinerary that includes Key West, Cozumel, Belize, New Orleans, and Galveston. She's in the luxury class, with one of the highest repeat passenger rates in the industry.

SeaEscape Cruises are inexpensive, one-day adventures to nowhere or to a brief call at Freeport in the Bahamas.

Silver Cloud and *Silver Wind* are Silversea Cruises' new (1994–1995), ultra-luxury-class ships that roam the world putting guests ashore in legendary ports to enjoy the most significant historical spots, the toniest restaurants, and uncrowded, offbeat tourism attractions. The five-star pampering is total from stem to stern, aboard and ashore.

Sun Fiesta ends up some days in the Bahamas and on other days cruises to "nowhere" to give passengers a taste of "love boat" activities and cuisine in a day cruise.

Westward is a Norwegian Cruise Line ship carrying 829 passengers on moderately priced three- and four-day cruises to the Bahamas and Key West, including a stop at the cruise line's private cay in the Bahamas.

Zenith is a high-moderate–class ship sailing the Caribbean on weeklong holidays. Her officers are Greek; her awards include a 1994 Golden Anchor for her price category.

FROM PALM BEACH

Crown Jewel, a Cunard Crown Cruise Lines ship, offers weeklong cruises of the Caribbean or Bahamas at high-moderate prices.

Viking Princess sails all day, every day. Some sailings are to Freeport in the Bahamas for a brief port of call; and others are out to sea so guests can enjoy the blue Atlantic.

FROM PORT CANAVERAL

Carnivale sails Thursdays for Nassau and Sundays for two ports in the Bahamas. Built in

1956 and known for almost nonstop music and entertainment, the ship is in the moderate price category.

Fantasy, the first superliner to come to Port Canaveral, can carry 2,600 passengers on three- and four-day cruises to the Bahamas. A Carnival Cruise Lines ship with rates in the moderate range, *Fantasy* also offers packages that include a stay in Orlando.

SeaEscape sails daily to see the sea all day, some days with a brief stop at Freeport, Grand Bahama. Although it's a budget-priced cruise experience, the ship has casinos, lavish buffets, and live entertainers.

Starship Atlantic and *Starship Oceanic* are perfect for families as well as for romantic couples or fun-loving singles. The children's programs are outstanding. Prices are in the moderate range.

FROM TAMPA

American Pioneer sails to the western Caribbean on weeklong adventures that specialize in **programs for families**, including special activities for children ages two to seventeen. Prices are in the low-moderate range, with a big discount on children's fares.

Gruziya, built in Finland, is a 400-passenger ship that once belonged to the Soviet Union. She sails weeklong cruises out of Tampa to the Yucatan and Honduras.

Nieuw Amsterdam is a comfortable Holland America ship that sails out of Tampa to Key West, Jamaica, Grand Cayman, and the Yucatan. Friendly Dutch officers and a hardworking Indonesian crew make for a happy ship with superb service, safety, and sightseeing. And this is one of the few cruise lines where tipping is not mandatory.

Regent Rainbow takes 960 passengers on a two-day, one-night cruise to nowhere each Friday and for five days in the Yucatan and Key West on Sundays. Prices are low to moderate.

StarShip Majestic sails on three- and four-day adventures complete with a full crew of Loony Tunes stars who will entertain the children, pose for pictures, and even sign autographs. The ports of call are exotic (Key West or Mexico), the children's programs outstanding, and the meals memorable. While this is one of the best family cruises afloat, it is equally suitable for singles and couples.

Tropicale is a 1,022-passenger Carnival Cruise Lines ship that sails seven-day cruises to Grand Cayman, the Yucatan, and New Orleans.

NORTHEAST FLORIDA

Emerald Princess sails out of downtown Amelia Island to the open sea, where she can throw open the slot machines and gaming tables. It's a good-time cruise with food, sunshine, dancing, showmanship, and sparkling seas. Waterfront, Fernandina Beach. 904-277-8980 or 800-842-0115.

Unusual Cruises

New on the Florida cruise scene is the *SSC Radisson Diamond*, an unusual catamaran-hull design that carries passengers in unusually stable comfort as well as lavish surroundings. Rates for the 177 cabins are in the luxury range. The ship's itinerary covers the world and includes Fort Lauderdale.

SMALL BOATS, SMALL HARBORS, BIG ADVENTURE

Nantucket Clipper is an intimate, 100-passenger ship that cruises the eastern seaboard from Maritime Canada to the Gulf of Mexico, usually offering one or two itineraries each year that include Florida. On a typical two-week cruise, ports of call include New Orleans, Biloxi, Pensacola, Tampa, Sanibel, the Marquesas, the Dry Tortugas, Key West, Miami, and Fort Lauderdale.

American-built, the ship draws only eight feet and has been outfitted specifically for regional cruising and small harbors, yet she has all the luxurious appointments and cuisine of a larger cruise ship. Staff naturalists are on hand to interpret the passing scene. Prices are in the high-moderate range. Book through your travel agent.

American Canadian Caribbean Line offers a unique Florida cruise experience as part of its restless roaming of the eastern seaboard, America's lakes and rivers, and the nearby Caribbean coasts and islands. Only a few cruises each year pass through Florida, so early planning is a must.

Part of the fun of these excursions is that you can stay aboard as long as you can afford to, cruising from here to there to there without seeing the same port twice. The other plus is the boats themselves. They are small enough to go into small ports that cruise liners cannot enter, yet large enough to offer cabins with private bathrooms, fine dining, and a friendly lounge with a money-saving BYOB policy. Except for shore tours, there are no extras.

While at anchor, you can fish or take out one of the small sailboats. The ships also carry a small glass-bottom boat and tenders. Designed for this service, the ships have bow ramps that make for easy embarkation/debarkation.

Florida ports of call include Palm Beach Gardens, Hobe Sound, Titusville, St. Augustine, Key West, Marathon, Cape Sable, Shark River and the Everglades, Indian Key, Marco Island, Fort Myers, Sanibel, La Costa, Sarasota, Carrabelle, Panama City, Fort Walton Beach, and Pensacola. Book through your travel agent or write American Canadian Caribbean Line, Box 368, Warren, RI 02885. 401-247-0955 (RI) or 800-556-7450 (United States and Canada).

PACKAGE DEALS

When booking any cruise, especially on a ship you'll live aboard, always ask about packages. Airfare add-on from most cities is usually much cheaper when booked with the cruise. Also available are pre- and post-cruise hotel accommodations ashore near the port, or complete tour packages (Orlando is the most common) that include rental car, accommodations, and perhaps some meals or tickets.

3 Lighthouses, Museums, Zoos, and Aquariums

LIGHTHOUSES

The lighthouses of Florida say more about man against man than about man against the sea. Although lights and towers had been used since the days of the earliest Spanish settlers, it wasn't until after the War of 1812 that our government became serious about fortifying its interests in the Gulf of Mexico. We had bested the British twice in wars; we had to be prepared for a third assault from them. We also had to protect American shipping against the pirates and freebooters who were terrorizing the Caribbean.

Good lighthouses were essential not just to the building and maintaining of the military outposts, but to counter the growing menace from professional wreckers, who set out false lights to lure ships onto the reefs. Others simply made deals with crooked captains, who would wreck their ships for a share of the booty.

Clearly, it was time for Uncle Sam to take charge. An obscure navy lieutenant named James Ramage suggested building a chain of lighthouses, and in the 1820s, Congress agreed. The Florida forts and lighthouses were to extend from Amelia Island in the far northeast corner of the state to Key West and the Dry Tortugas, and up the west coast to Pensacola.

During the Civil War, lighthouses came under fire off and on; nobody was quite sure whether to let them shine or not. Blockade running was important to the South, whose only manufactured goods were coming from Europe via the Bahamas and Bermuda. Catching blockade runners was important to the North, which also needed the lighthouses to guide its own gunboats and supply ships. So lighthouses became prizes of war, even though combatants couldn't always agree on whether they would be better off to darken them or light them.

Some of the state's most scenic lighthouses are listed below. Keep in mind that climbing any of them is strenuous exercise, often in very warm temperatures and steambath humidity, and usually on narrow, metal stairs. Don't try it if you're not in good shape.

Now an automatic light, **Amelia Island Lighthouse** has been in continuous operation since 1839, sending a beam sixteen miles out to sea from the second highest elevation on the Atlantic coast. Located in a residential neighborhood of Fernandina Beach, the lighthouse is not open to the public, nor is it

accessible. However, it can be captured in photographs from afar to add to your collection.

Part of Cape Florida State Recreation Area, the **Cape Florida Lighthouse** is the oldest building in South Florida. It also has one of the most exciting histories. In 1836, during the second Seminole war, the lighthouse was attacked by Indians. Keepers fled to the top of the light, where, in desperation, they rolled a keg of gunpowder down the stairs and blew the attackers away. One of the defenders was killed. The other escaped to a ship offshore, but the burned-out lighthouse was abandoned to the Indians. It was rebuilt in 1846 and in 1855 was raised from sixty-five to ninety-five feet.

Early in the Civil War, the light was again the scene of drama when three southern sympathizers talked their way into the lighthouse, which was occupied by the Union. They smashed the lens and took the lamps, snuffing an important beacon used by the blockade runners that could have helped their own cause. The South reactivated the light, only to have it shelled by offshore Federal ships. As a beacon, it was replaced in 1878 by the Fowey Rock Light.

Bill Baggs Cape Florida State Recreation

Area, 1200 South Crandon Boulevard, Key Biscayne, Miami. 305-361-5811. State park admissions apply. The park is open from 8:00 A.M. to sunset daily.

Cape St. George Light, an automatic light, provides a salty backdrop for photos of Little St. George Island, which is accessible only by boat. The lighthouse is at the western end of St. George Island, which has a state park. Little St. George Island is off Apalachicola.

Egmont Key is not the most picturesque lighthouse in Florida, but it's the only man-managed lighthouse left in the United States. Accessible only by boat, 440-acre Egmont Key was a prison camp for Seminoles captured during the Indian Wars. During the Civil War, it was a Union stronghold. Egmont Key is located at the mouth of Tampa Bay, southwest of Desoto Beach. 813-893-2627.

One of the most photographed lighthouses in the state, **Jupiter Inlet Lighthouse** is located in a picturesque little lagoon surrounded by marinas and waterfront restaurants. Built in 1860 and the oldest structure in the county, this mellow red beacon is still a working lighthouse maintained by the U.S. Coast Guard.

Try to get a close look at the bull's-eye lens, which is crisscrossed with bars. It was blown out during a hurricane in 1928. Broken pieces were rounded up, sent to Charleston, and reassembled with the help of the metal supports.

Jupiter Inlet Lighthouse, Alternate State A1A, Jupiter, at Jupiter Inlet. 407-747-6639.

The museum is open for only a few hours on Sundays; admission is free.

The only American lighthouse located in the center of a city, the 110-foot **Key West Lighthouse** was built in 1846 to replace a light that was built in 1825 and destroyed in the 1846 hurricane. Today the lighthouse and the meticulously restored keeper's cottage form a superb museum.

Plan to spend a couple of hours here to tour the comfortable cottage with its heart pine floors and cypress paneling, a very good collection of memorabilia and artifacts, and the lushly tropical grounds. Then climb the lighthouse for a fine view of the surrounding sea and city.

Key West Lighthouse, 938 Whitehead Street. 305-294-0012. Open daily except Christmas. Admission fee.

Everyone calls it simply Ponce Inlet, a deep-

Jupiter Inlet Lighthouse is one of the most photographed in the state

water ocean inlet that streams day and night with fleets of colorful fishing boats inbound and outbound. It's a great hangout, with rustic bars and seafood restaurants. Crowning it all is **Ponce de Leon Inlet Lighthouse**, a 175-foot red landmark lighthouse completed in 1887. Once deactivated, it has been restored and put back into service as a working beacon.

Puff your way up the 203 steps to the top for a panoramic view of the Atlantic to the east and the Intracoastal Waterway and neighborhoods to the west. Bring a picnic to enjoy in the adjacent park if you like, and take time to explore some of the old ruins around the grounds. Nature trails, picnic areas, showers, and rest rooms are available, and the fishing jetty is wheelchair accessible. A small fee is charged to tour the lighthouse.

Ponce de Leon Inlet Lighthouse, 4931 South Peninsula Drive, Ponce Inlet. 904-761-1821. Open from 10:00 A.M. daily; closings vary according to the season. Closed Christmas.

St. Johns Lighthouse, located on the Mayport Naval Air Station, is part of the American Lighthouse Museum at 1011 North Third Street in Jacksonville Beach. The museum is open Tuesday through Saturday from 10:00 A.M. to 5:00 P.M. 904-241-8845. The naval station is open to the public on weekends, and at least one ship is usually open for tours.

Most of Florida's lighthouse legends read like historical romances, but the **Lighthouse Museum** of St. Augustine has a high-tech twist. A landmark of some kind has marked the place sailors call Crazy Banks since the late 1500s, when the Spanish built a watchtower. In 1824, when a lens was added, it became Florida's first official lighthouse.

A grand lighthouse with a 20,000-candle-power Fresnel lens was completed in 1874. Then, in 1986, Floridians were horrified to learn that a vandal with a high-powered rifle had damaged 14 of the 320 precious prisms. The Coast Guard wanted to replace the Fresnel with a modern beacon until St. Augustine citizens rose up, raised $55,000, and scoured the world to find a company capable of doing this lost-art repair work. In succeeding, they rewrote the book on lighthouse repair.

Lens components had been made in France specifically for the lighthouse. Although lenses look similar, restorers soon learned that no two

Fresnel lenses are identical. Each lighthouse was an assembly of custom pieces put together in a specific order. Many bits and pieces had been salvaged from decommissioned Fresnel lighthouses around the nation, but none fit the nine-foot, first-order beacon here. And nobody knew how to make new ones. Atlantic Industrial Optics of Georgetown, Delaware, was brought in on the case. The project proved so interesting that the local Junior Service League gave a lantern and lens repair workshop that was attended by representatives from fifteen states.

The restored lighthouse was rededicated in 1993. The complex includes a small museum, lighthouse keeper's quarters, and a park with nature trails in a setting of dunes and live oaks.

81 Lighthouse Avenue, on Anastasia Island; 904-829-0745. Admission is charged. The lighthouse is open daily except major holidays.

MARITIME MUSEUMS, AQUARIUMS, AND ATTRACTIONS

Aqua Trek's Sealife Learning Center is the only oceanarium in this part of Florida, and it features the area's largest touch tank. With marine biologist Carl Melamet, you'll discover the undersea world of Sanibel Island and Pine Island Sound both in the center and on excursions into the surrounding seas. The center is at 2353 Periwinkle Way, Sanibel (reached via toll causeway from Fort Myers). 813-472-8680.

Bailey-Matthews Shell Museum is rightly placed on Sanibel Island, which has some of the best shelling in the United States. Thousands of common and rare shells attract sightseers, as well as serious collectors, from all over the world. More than 275 kinds of shells are found in shallow waters of Sanibel and Captiva; another 500 varieties are found offshore in the Gulf. Call 813-395-2233 for information. At press time a new museum is being built.

The **Clearwater Marine Science Center and Aquarium** is a fine little museum where you'll see living marine life and models. It's also a rehab center for injured marine life and a nursery for baby turtles. 249 Wildward Passage, Clearwater, 813-441-1790. Admission is charged. Open Monday through Friday from 9:00 A.M. to 5:00 P.M., Saturday from 9:00 A.M. to 4:00 P.M., and Sunday from 11:00 A.M. to 4:00 P.M.

The **Florida Aquarium** is a massive project built on 4.3 acres where Garrison and Ybor channels come together in downtown Tampa. Plan to spend at least one full day in one of the nation's largest and most modern aquariums. (The grand opening is planned for April 1995.) It's a find for anyone who loves seas and shores; for those with a special interest in Florida waters, it's a major discovery.

Touring the three-level complex under a great glass ceiling in the shape of a seashell, visitors will follow a drop of water from the time it leaves the freshwater springs and limestone caves of a Florida aquifer through rivers and wetlands to the beaches and open seas.

Major habitats will show springs and wetlands, a bay and barrier beaches, a coral reef, and the Gulf Stream and open sea. Each will contain appropriate marine life, more than 4,300 animals and plants representing 550 species that are native to Florida.

You'll walk through the sawgrass marsh to see alligator hatchings, an otter's den, and a cypress swamp. Then you'll meet the sea in the tangled roots of mangrove thickets. Next, you'll see the beach and bay, shellfish and rays playing in simulated waves, and even a bridge that demonstrates man's impact on the environment.

The Florida Aquarium's signature exhibit will be the coral reef, where visitors will pass through a see-through tunnel into a world of staghorn coral, brilliant reef fish, and, finally, a coral cave.

As visitors enter the Gulf Stream, with its jellyfish and sargasso weed, they will come into the open ocean with its sharks and pelagic fish.

Downtown Tampa in Garrison Seaport Center. 800-448-2672 or 813-229-8861. Admission is charged.

The venerable **Gulfarium** is to Fort Walton Beach what Marineland is to the east coast of Florida—a time-honored marine attraction featuring trained porpoises, whales, otters, a petting pool, harbor seals, and alligators. Adding to the color are a colony of penguins and a display of tropical birds. 1010 Miracle Strip Parkway S.E., Fort Walton Beach. 904-244-5169. Open daily except on Thanksgiving and Christmas.

At the **Harbor Branch Oceanographic Research Center**, the operative word is research, so this is less a tourist attraction than a sharing in important, deep-water research.

Founded in 1971 by Link Trainer pioneer Ed Link and funded by Johnson & Johnson, the center operates highly sophisticated deep-sea diving equipment and submersibles, including the famous Johnson Sea-Link.

The more you know about oceanography and related sciences, the better you'll understand and appreciate the displays here. Although there are displays for all levels, including children, adults and young people will appreciate them most. On exhibit are relics from the *Monitor*, a Civil War gunship salvaged by the Link team.

North of Fort Pierce on US 1. 305-465-2400. Hours are Monday through Friday from 10:30 A.M. to 3:00 P.M.

At the **Manatee Observatory and Educational Center**, you'll see manatee in their natural surroundings as they munch vegetation, nurse their young, and give you a curious look as they come up for air. Downtown Fort Pierce on the Indian River. 407-466-3880. At press time, the observatory was still under construction. (Groundbreaking is planned for October 1994.)

Lowry Park Zoo is one of the largest zoos in North America. Located in Tampa, it has an Asian domain, a petting zoo, a good selection of Florida wildlife, and all the attributes of a fine zoo. Of special interest is the **Manatee Aquatic Center** with its population of endangered manatee. A coral reef exhibit is interesting, too. 7530 North Boulevard, Tampa. 813-935-8552. Admission is charged. Wheelchairs and strollers are available for rent. Open daily from 9:30 A.M. to 5:00 P.M.

Marineland isn't as slick as some of the newer theme parks in Florida, but it was the first, and that's part of its charm. So is its waterfront location on the coastal highway (State A1A) just south of St. Augustine. This is unhurried, old Florida, worlds apart from the jangle and crowding of the theme parks.

Feed a dolphin, pet a starfish, and laugh at sea lion antics. See tanks of sharks, rays, moray eels, and toothy barracuda. The seashell museum here is one of the most comprehensive in the nation.

Between St. Augustine and Daytona Beach on State A1A. 800-824-4218 or 904-471-1111. A Quality Inn and a campground are located on the site, which has a superb beach and restaurants, including the Dolphin, which has an ocean view. One admission fee covers for all shows and exhibits, all day.

Watch manatees in their natural surroundings

Juno Beach, near Stuart, is the home of the **Marinelife Center**, an excellent little museum filled with aquariums and exhibits. Many of the displays center on sea turtles, which nest on these beaches. Admission is free, but donations are appreciated. 1200 US 1, Loggerhead Park, Juno Beach. 407-627-8280. Open Tuesday through Saturday from 10:00 A.M. to 3:00 P.M., Sunday from noon to 3:00 P.M.

The **McLarty Treasure Museum** is devoted to the tradition of treasure hunting. In 1715, an entire fleet of Spanish treasure ships went down off Melbourne, and it was here, at Sebastian Inlet, that Spanish salvors set up camp soon afterward. With their primitive equipment they were able to save only some of the treasure. Modern salvagers with more sophisticated equipment continue to find more relics, and even beachcombers find the occasional piece of eight. Sebastian Inlet State Recreation Area, 9700 South A1A, Melbourne Beach. 407-984-4852.

The home of television's Flipper, **Miami Seaquarium** is located in a fifty-acre tropical garden. View dolphins underwater, explore the tide pool touch tank, and applaud the sea lion and dolphin shows, which run all day,

every day. One admission fee covers all the shows. It's at the Rickenbacker Causeway. 305-361-5705.

The best feature of the **Mote Marine Aquarium** is a 135,000-gallon outdoor tank filled with sharks. In a small tank are creatures you're welcome to touch. Florida marine creatures you'll see include sea turtles, living sponges, coral, fish of all kinds, and octopus. 1600 Thompson Parkway, Sarasota. 813-388-4441. Admission is charged. Open daily except major holidays, 10:00 A.M. to 5:00 P.M.

At the **Museum of Man and the Sea**, a one-of-a-kind museum, you'll see relics from the earliest days of diving, wreck diving, and underwater exploration. Start with the twenty-four-minute video, which explains the history of undersea adventure, including the training taken by astronauts to accustom them to weightlessness. On display are artifacts and treasures dating to the sixteenth century. US 98, just west of State 79 in Panama City Beach. Open daily from 9:00 A.M. to 5:00 P.M. 800-PC-BEACH or 904-233-6503.

Ocean World is a compact but action-packed marine attraction in the heart of Fort Lauderdale, where continuous shows feature dolphins, sea lions, and exotic birds. For one admission price, you can stay as long as you like. Optional is a one-hour narrated cruise of the Intracoastal Waterway. 701 S.E. 17th Street Causeway, Fort Lauderdale. 305-525-6612. Open daily.

The largest display of naval aviation equipment in the world, the **Pensacola National Museum of Naval Aviation** has an Underwater Recovery Exhibit that will interest divers as well as pilots. Two World War II–era navy aircraft that were recovered from Lake Michigan are displayed in a simulated underwater environment. They've been left just as they were found, giving the scene an eerie, authentic look and feel.

Also on display is the only remaining Douglas NC-4, one of four enormous four-engined flying boats that set off to fly around the world in 1919. With one boat already damaged in a fire, the other three took off from Rockaway, New York. One had to land at sea and "taxi" for two and a half days to make safe harbor in the Azores. Only this one completed the record-making circumnavigation.

In Pensacola, follow signs to the Naval Air Station, then to the museum. 904-453-2389.

Admission is free. The museum is open daily from 9:00 A.M. to 5:00 P.M.

At **Turtle Kraals of Key West**, turtles were once penned and slaughtered. This historic site on Key West's docks is now the home of the Florida Marine Conservancy. Sea turtles, sea birds, and other sick and injured marine creatures are brought here for treatment and rehabilitation. It's worth seeing both for the good work that's being done and for the historic site. Land's End Village, Key West. 305-294-2640. Open Monday through Friday from 11:00 A.M. to 1:00 P.M. only, all year. Admission is free.

The Pier in St. Petersburg is a waterfront landmark with a sensational view of Tampa Bay, the historic Vinoy Hotel (now stunningly restored as a Stouffer resort), and miles of grassy parks in downtown St. Pete. Here in one complex you can shop, dine indoors or out in a choice of restaurants, and see one of the state's best small aquariums. 800 Second Avenue N.E., St. Petersburg. 813-821-6164. Park anywhere on the one-quarter-mile-long causeway; a free shuttle bus will take you to the Pier. The Pier is open daily; the aquarium is closed Tuesdays.

Living Seas at Walt Disney World's EPCOT

Center combines a high-tech aquarium with high-velocity entertainment as only the Imagineers of WDW can do. The largest facility ever dedicated to man's relationship with the seas, it's a six-million-gallon "ocean" filled with living sea creatures of all kinds. A total seawater environment, it is 200 feet in diameter and 27 feet deep.

Here you'll see sharks and triggerfish swimming in lazy harmony with jacks, dolphins, snappers, angelfish, brightly colored parrot fish, and human scuba divers. Guests enter the Living Seas at a 185-seat theater, where they are shown a seven-minute film about the ocean. They then descend into Sea Base Alpha, a twenty-first-century research center where scientists are studying the ocean.

If you make reservations early, you can dine in the Living Seas Restaurant, with a huge glass window on the undersea world. The food and ambience are in the "fine dining" class, so allow time and budget for a unique meal.

Living Seas is one of the pavilions at EPCOT Center, Walt Disney World. Single and multiday passes are sold. 407-824-4321.

Sea World of Florida is not only one of the best aquatic theme parks in the United States, it's an important marine life research, rescue, and rehabilitation center. Plan to spend at least one whole day, preferably two, to see all the shows and exhibits. In Shark Encounter, you are surrounded by sharks as you walk a tunnel in an enormous see-through tank. In Penguin Encounter, you'll see penguins going about their everyday lives above and below the water.

Terrors of the Deep is one of the world's biggest assemblies of stinging, biting, mauling sea creatures. Shamu the killer whale puts on a breathtaking show. Another exhibit, titled Manatee, The Last Generation, is a poignant look at the ugly, ungainly, lovable sea cow that is fast disappearing from Florida waters. Entertainment throughout Sea World is fast-paced and lavish, with waterski shows, a jolting ride deep in the Bermuda Triangle, and a laser light spectacular. Shamu's Happy Harbor is three acres of playground fun for the children; the Polynesian Luau is feasting and fun for the whole family.

7007 Sea World Drive, Orlando; 407-351-3600. Admission rates are all-inclusive, comparable to those at Universal Studios and Walt Disney World. Ask about multiple-day passes.

Restaurants and snack bars are found throughout the grounds; for the Polynesian Revue, reservations are required.

A trip to **Suncoast Seabird Sanctuary**, one of the largest wild bird treatment centers in the nation, is a heart-tugging experience. Late every afternoon, buckets of fish are brought out to the shore to feed seabirds. Because they know they can get a meal here, many of those that show up are the day's casualties—birds that are caught in tangles of fishing line, stuck with a fishhook, or caught in a plastic sixpack ring. Without help, they would face a lingering, painful death.

Loving hands capture the birds, fix them up, and send them on their way. Most are treated on the spot, in the few seconds it takes to remove a hook. Others must be treated and rehabilitated. Although pelicans seem to predominate, staff members have helped more than seventy-five types of birds here.

Suncoast Seabird Sanctuary is located at 18328 Gulf Boulevard (State 699) in Indian Shores, on the ocean west of St. Petersburg. 813-391-6211. Admission is free, but donations are welcome. Guided tours are given on Wednesday and Sunday afternoons.

Weeki Wachee Spring is one of Florida's oldest attractions, where mermaids have been performing underwater ballets since 1947 in a clear spring bubbling with brilliant bursts of air. The show is natural and nostalgic, performed in the world's largest underwater theater.

Admission covers a day of shows and exhibits. See the mermaid show, a superb display of birds of prey, a petting zoo, and gardens and shops. Also included in the admission is a cruise on the Weeki Wachee River to the pelican orphanage.

On State 50 at the junction of US 19, 12 miles west of Brooksville. 813-596-2062 or 800-678-9335. Open daily. Buccaneer Bay, a water theme park next door, is a good place to cool off. Combination tickets are a good buy.

OTHER NAUT-WORTHY ATTRACTIONS

You'll surely see plenty of alligators in the wild if you take many of the nature cruises listed in this book, but a visit to the historic **Alligator Farm** is also worthwhile. Established in 1893, the attraction focuses more now on nature and wildlife preservation than on the hokey showmanship that Florida tourists once expected.

You'll see alligators, turtles, and reptiles in scheduled shows. Walk the boardwalk through a swamp that teems with gators and exotic birds. Then stop by the pool where Gomek, a 17.5-foot-long New Guinea crocodile, holds court. Spend all day for one admission charge. South of St. Augustine on State A1A. 904-824-3337. Open daily from 9:00 A.M. to 5:00 P.M.

Cypress Gardens, one of Florida's most beloved tourist attractions since the 1930s, brings its beauty into the slick Disney era without losing any of its disarming, old-Florida charm. The 223-acre park, now one of the state's major theme parks, was built around lakes rimmed with cypress trees, sliver-size waterways that thread through stunning gardens, and vast lawns studded with gardens and statuary.

One price covers all-day admission to all the cruises and attractions, including the world-famous waterski shows, museums, a bird show, a model railroad, and much more. Cruises include the whisper-quiet electric boat ride as well as pontoon boat rides. Just as they have for

generations, Southern belles in hoop skirts stroll the grounds, happy to pose for your camera.

Cypress Gardens is located four miles southwest of Winter Haven on State 540. 813-324-2111. Open daily.

Special note: Cold snaps can hit this part of Florida in winter, but Cypress Gardens spends a fortune on heaters that keep its priceless tropical plantings alive. Even during years when the occasional big freeze hits central Florida, you can count on getting your money's worth here.

Eckerd College overlooks Boca Ciega Bay, so it's only natural that boating is part of campus life. Athletics include windsurfing and sailing—the college has forty-five sailboats—and an elaborate, all-volunteer search and rescue program in which students are prepared to drop everything and take to the water when anyone sends a Mayday. If you're looking for a college education with a minor in boating, tour this campus. Older people can also attend Eckerd's frequent and superb seaside Elderhostels. 4200 54th Avenue South, St. Petersburg, FL 33711. 813-864-8256 or 800-451-3212.

International Swimming Hall of Fame is a

huge complex where you can swim in an Olympic pool and/or tour a museum devoted to swimming and diving history, stars, and art. There's also a good library devoted to swimming subjects. 1 Hall of Fame Drive, Fort Lauderdale. 305-462-6536. Admission is charged. Open daily.

Lummus Park on the Miami River makes it easier to imagine what pioneer life would have been like when rivers were the state's inland highways, before Miami became the metropolis it is today. Fort Dallas, which operated from 1835 to 1838, has been rebuilt here. It was once under the command of William Tecumseh Sherman, who went on to fame in the Civil War. Also open to tours is the Wagner House, one of the oldest pioneer homes in the area. 404 N.W. North River Drive at N.W. Third Street, Miami. 305-575-5240. Open daily; free.

Naval Live Oaks Reservation. If old wooden ships strike your fancy, you've probably already noticed that the enormous live oak trees of Florida, sculpted by lashing sea winds, have grown into shapes that are perfectly formed to make ribs and knees for huge ships. So important were these strong, naturally bent trees to early

America that live oak forests were fought over by the Spanish and the English, then by the English and the Americans, all of them eager to harvest the trees to build warships.

By the 1820s, it occurred to some naval supplier that the trees should be farmed like any other commodity. In an odd footnote to history, calculations were made to determine how many trees would be used to build how many ships, and the right number of acorns were planted near Pensacola in a small community named Gulf Breeze.

Legend says that live oaks take 200 years to grow, 200 to live, and 200 to die, but tree farmers were counting on a usable crop within 50 years. Unfortunately for them, tree thieves ran off with some of the oaks to sell to foreign navies, and, by the 1870s, when the crop was at its best, iron warships had been proven in battle and the live oaks were no longer of interest.

The visitors center is located on US 98 about a mile east of Gulf Breeze. Exhibits explain the history of the reservation. It's open daily from 8:30 A.M. to 5:00 P.M. The plantation is open from 8:00 A.M. to sunset. Free. 904-932-7888.

Underwater Demolition Team–SEAL Museum is devoted to the history of frogmen, sea commandos, and other underwater specialists. It all began here in 1943, with the training of frogmen during World War II. 3300 North State A1A, Fort Pierce. 407-489-3597. Open Tuesday through Saturday, 10:00 A.M. to 4:00 P.M.; Sunday, noon to 4:00 P.M. Free.

Universal Studios' "Jaws!" attraction is more terrifying than the movie because you're almost caught in the snapping jaws of a thirty-two-foot monster before an explosion in which the shark is killed. Jaws dies while passengers are rocked, knocked, singed by the explosion, and scared silly.

The ride is the highlight of a section of the studios that is old Cape Cod down to the last shingle. Because this is a working movie studio, you'll often see filmings taking place here and in the theme park's many other realistic sets. All-day admission includes rides, shows, and all attractions. 1000 Universal Studios Plaza, Orlando. 407-363-8000.

ABOUT HANDICAPPED ACCESS

Because of the nature of some seagoing and shoreside listings throughout this book, wheelchair access may be limited or may require advance planning. Call ahead.

Nature Cruises

CHARLOTTE HARBOR

King Fisher Cruises sail out of Fisherman's Village in search of seashells by the seashore. Schedules vary, but this is a year-round operation. 1200 West Retta Esplanade, Punta Gorda. 813-639-0969.

CRYSTAL SPRINGS

Oceanic Society Expeditions of San Francisco offers a five-day expedition in which participants observe and swim with manatees in Crystal Bay,

north of Tampa. Here, powerful springs rise out of the ocean floor, spilling fresh water into the salt water of the Gulf of Mexico. Because the water temperature is constant all year, it's a popular playground for sea cows, or manatees. The package begins and ends in Fort Lauderdale. Accommodations, land transportation, and boat trips are included. 800-326-7491 or 415-441-1106.

DAYTONA BEACH

Speed out into the open Atlantic off Daytona Beach aboard the **Sea Critter**, a 2,160-horsepower "rocketship" that is billed as the world's fastest 130-passenger speedboat. Once at sea you'll watch for dolphins, whales, and seabirds while getting a good view of the seacoast. The Critter Fleet docks across from the Ponce Inlet Lighthouse south of Daytona Beach. 904-767-7676.

DRY TORTUGAS

Mere crumbs of islands deep in the Gulf of Mexico seventy miles west of Key West, the Dry Tortugas are a favorite resting stop for migrating birds en route to and from Central and South America. Because they're so remote—accessible only by boat or seaplane—the islands provide a privileged look at a wealth of birds in a breeze-swept island setting visited only by the most persistent nature watchers.

Florida Nature Tours makes only a few voyages each year to the Tortugas, leaving Key West at 11:00 P.M. and arriving at Bird Garden Key just before dawn. On board with the forty passengers for the three-day cruise are half a dozen qualified naturalists who will point out terns, frigate birds, boobies, storm petrels, tropical birds, sooty terns (for which this is a major

nesting ground), and many more varieties. Box 5643, Winter Park, FL 32793-5643. 407-273-4400.

A classic glass-bottom boat that has been around Key West since the 1950s, *Fireball* is the perfect vessel for viewing the living reef from the lower deck or watching the bird life from a sunny top deck. Narrated, two-hour cruises sail twice a day from Fireball Dock between Pier House and Ocean Key House, on the water off Front Street between Simonton and Duval. 305-296-6293 or 305-294-8704.

M/V *Discovery* lets you watch through big glass windows as the ship glides through reefs abounding with colorful fish and brilliant coral. The ship sails three times each day, with hours varying in winter and summer. Get tickets at Land's End Village, 251 Margaret Street, Key West, and they'll direct you to the dock. Call for reservations. 305-293-0099.

ESTERO BAY

Sail out of Bonita Springs into the shining bay that was once home to the Calusa Indians. As you keep a lookout for manatee, dolphin, gulls, and sea hawks, you'll learn how the Calusas constructed the shell midden mounds that have turned many of these low barrier islands into impressive hills. Off US 41 in Bonita Springs, take Coconut Road to the end. Contact Estero Bay Boat Tours about the three daily cruises. 813-992-2200.

THE EVERGLADES

The Everglades form the second largest national park in the United States. At first look, the steamy, low-lying, seemingly featureless 'Glades are no competition for the snowcapped mountains and towering redwoods of the national parks in the West. It takes time and patience to discover that this is nature's drama at its kindest and most cruel. The Everglades teem with life all year: waterfowl snatching fingerling fish from their reed beds, osprey swooping from the sky to carry off small animals, alligators lying slyly in wait for unwary prey. Wild orchids cling to trees; islands turn white each night as egrets come home to roost. A few Florida panthers, almost extinct, hunt by night. Deer browse in the hammocks. Black bears occasionally bumble into view. Raccoons, curious and hungry, raid campsites.

Babcock Wilderness Adventures is a swamp buggy tour through the 90,000-acre Babcock Ranch and the Telegraph Cypress Swamp. Naturalists are there to explain the unique ecosystem of southern Florida. You're sure to see clouds of big, flappy birds, flocks of songbirds, and probably alligators, raccoons, and swamp life of all kinds. Trips leave from State 31 in Punta Gorda. 813-338-6367.

Collier-Seminole State Park covers 6,423 acres of grasslands, mangrove swamp, rare Florida royal palm, picturesque hammocks, pine flatwoods, and saltmarshes. It's home to a world of threatened and endangered wildlife, including panthers, manatees, wood storks, bald eagles, brown pelicans, Florida black bears, and the American crocodile. Boat tours are narrated by park rangers. The park is located on US 41, seventeen miles south of Naples. 813-394-3397.

The Conservancy Inc. in Naples consists of a natural science museum with serpentarium, a wildlife clinic, a nature store, and naturalist-narrated boat tours of the Gordon River; 813-262-0304. The Conservancy's **Nature Center** on Shell Island Road off State 951, six miles north of Marco, offers boat tours of Rookery Bay.

They're led by naturalists who know every inch of these unique, estuarine backwaters, and they'll point out oyster bars, red-breasted mergansers, scrub jays, and snowy egrets. Small islands just off Marco Island are considered the largest wading bird rookery in the state. 813-775-8569.

Everglades Holiday Park Airboat Tours skim through the Everglades to a Seminole Indian village. The world's largest airboat, *Big Foot* departs from Griffin Road, a half mile west of US 27, Fort Lauderdale. 305-438-8111.

Everglades Institute, off US 41 (Tamiami Trail), offers airboat and swamp buggy cruises that are led by biologists. 813-695-3143.

Everglades Jungle Cruises sail out of the city yacht basin at the end of Lee Street in Fort Myers for a three-hour cruise of the jungle-lined Caloosahatchee River. 813-334-7474.

Island Nature Cruises out of Port of the Islands explore the huge buffer zone, known as the 10,000 Islands, where freshwater drainage from the land forms a unique environment as it joins the salt sea. A giant nursery for bird life ashore on the mangrove islands and sea life in the soup-warm waters, it's a wildlife watcher's delight.

Two-hour cruises leave from Marina Chickee Hut, site of Naples' only manatee sanctuary, on US 41 (Tamiami Trail) about twenty miles east of Naples and eighty miles west of Miami. 813-394-3101 or 800-237-4173.

Jet Airboat Adventure has five boats, all of them able to skim over the swamps and grasses of the Everglades to take you to an Indian village and an alligator farm. Professional guides are on board to explain the unique ecology of the area and to point out egrets, heron, alligators, and plant life. Boats launch from Everglades City, thirty-five miles south of Naples at the end of State 29. 800-282-9194.

Majestic Tours are a project of Frank and Georgia Garrett, who specialize in the western portion of Everglades National Park. Their forty-mile cruise through the mangroves lasts three and a half to four hours. Find them at historic Smallwood's Store on Chokoloskee Island, ten miles from Everglades City. Take State 29 south from US 41. 813-695-2777.

Miccosukee Indian Village and Airboat Rides is based at Mile Marker 40, US 41 west of Miami. Visit the heart of the Everglades to see

Pelicans are always fun to watch

how native peoples live, then let one of them guide your airboat tour through the 'Glades. 305-223-8380 or 223-8388.

Western Water Gateway is the northwest corner of Everglades National Park, on the Chokoloskee Causeway of State 29. From here, boat tours of the Wilderness Waterway leave the park's docks. 813-695-2591.

Wooten's has been zooming airboats and swamp buggies through the most remote wilds of the western Everglades since 1953. You'll swoop through grasses and mangroves, across lakes and islands, past strangler fig trees and palm hammocks hung with wild orchids. During the Seminole wars, canoes of warriors hid in these creeks and sloughs. Today they're the lair of alligators and the nearly extinct Florida panther, as well as snowy egrets and great blue herons. Wooten's is located on US 41, thirty-five miles south of Naples at Ochopee (the nation's smallest post office). 800-282-2781.

Gentle manatees are dying by the dozens everywhere in Florida after they tangle with boat propellers. **Homosassa Springs State Wildlife Park** is one of their refuges, and visitors can view the gentle giants in their underwater world. The park also has a manatee rehabilitation center, an extensive collection of native Florida birds and animals, and nature shows. Boat tours of the fifty-five-foot-deep spring and the river it pours into are offered daily. The park is located at 9225 West Fish Bowl Drive, Homosassa. 904-628-2311.

Although **Lake Griffin State Recreation Area** is only an hour from Orlando's razzle-dazzle attractions, this sprawling lake just south of Ocala National Forest is a world apart. A paddle wheel on the small excursion boat adds to the fun of nature cruises. You'll see a wealth of bird life, from stalking shorebirds to big-winged anhingas, egrets, herons, and cormorants. Nature trips sail periodically from 7:00 A.M. to 5:00 P.M. daily, and sometimes at night. Off US 27 on Picciola Road in Fruitland Park. 904-787-4916.

A forty-six-passenger boat sails daily into **Lake Okeechobee**, a fascinating, little-known Florida lake, the second largest lake totally within the United States. Naturalist narrators trained by the National Audubon Society take you back to the time when Florida belonged to storks and egrets, snakes and eagles, alligator and ibis, and the prehistoric Indians that hunted them. Side trips include a swamp buggy tour to a nearby

Clewiston docks near Lake Okeechobee

"cracker" ranch, where a camp dinner is served. On State 78 west in Okeechobee at the Kissimmee River Bridge. 813-467-4411.

Boat tours in **Myakka River State Park** take wildlife seekers along the twelve miles of river that flow through this 28,875-acre state park. See oak palm hammocks, grassy swamps atwitter with bird and insect life, and sloughs that cut through island rookeries that are sometimes so thickly covered with birds you can hardly see the trees. Cruise through prairie landscape and into pine woods, where you'll see deer, cottontail, wild turkeys, alligators, and hawks. The park is twelve miles east of Sarasota on State 72. 813-361-6511.

REEF ROAMING

Increasingly threatened by pollution, anchors, and other intrusion, living coral reefs are ever harder to find in the United States, but miles of them are found off southeast Florida and the Keys. The 2,700 nautical square miles that surround them form the **Florida Keys National Marine Sanctuary**.

Biscayne National Underwater Park is 180,000 acres of water, reefs, and islands. Park rangers on glass-bottom boats explain reef life as you glide over a living aquarium. Guided canoe tours are also offered. The tour boat office is in Homestead. 305-247-2400.

John Pennekamp Coral Reef State Park covers 53,661 acres of coral reefs, beds of seagrass, and mangrove swamps surrounded by 2,350 acres of land that hosts many rare and endangered plants. Aboard a glass-bottom boat trip over the reefs you could see almost anything from sharks and manta rays to grouper, jewfish, schools of brilliant reef fish, sea turtles, and coral fans. Mangrove islands serve as a nursery for small fish that dart among tangled mangrove roots. At the waterline, watch for coon oysters that cling to the roots and provide dinner for shorebirds and raccoons. It's a cruise to take time and again because nature writes the script, and it's unpredictable. The park is at MM 201.5 north of Key Largo. 305-451-1202.

MANGROVE ROAMING

In a **Mangrove Safari** out of Sugarloaf Key (MM 17), you'll board a stable, sea-kindly, twenty-

Roam the reefs

four-foot Carolina Skiff to skim the backcountry of the Florida Keys. Captains Gale and Bobby Dumouchel wind you through mangrove mazes, where the trees' root communities teem with snapper and coon oysters. You'll wade tidal flats, snorkel over seagrass, and scan the treetops for birds on the edge of the Gulf of Mexico in the Great White Heron National Wildlife Refuge. At T. J. Sugarshack Marina, MM 17, Lower Sugarloaf Key. 305-745-2868. Half-day excursions accommodate no more than six persons.

Special note: bring polarized sunglasses, protective footwear, sunscreen, and towels. Snacks, beverages, and fresh fruit are served on board.

Hawk's Cay Ecology Tours leave from the marina at this exclusive resort on Duck Key for a two-hour interpretive tour of a nearby, uninhabited island. The tour does not go every day. Call 305-743-7000 for schedules.

A three-hour round-trip boat tour departs from Indian Key to **Lignumvitae Key State Botanical Site**, a 280-acre island, Thursday through Monday. Once you reach the island, a guide will walk you through a majestic tropical forest of gumbo-limbo, Jamaica dogwood, mastic, poisonwood, strangler fig, and the rare lignumvitae, a wood so hard it will neither float nor burn. Once overharvested for use as bearings and other shipbuilding purposes, it is now protected. Call for reservations and instructions. 305-451-7617.

THE DOLPHIN CONNECTION

Cruising anywhere in Florida waters, you're likely to spot a pod of dolphins who come along for the ride. It may just be our imagination, but we're convinced that they're attracted by the sound of a boat's engine, and they truly want to join the fun. It's a delight to watch them dance and dive in the boat's wake while they grin up at you.

Dolphins are found in petting pools at some marine attractions, and at some places you can swim with them. Advance reservations are a must. The following locales accent dolphins.

Dolphins Plus on Key Largo is more a research center than an entertainment, but visitors are invited to participate in dolphin programs if they are experienced swimmers. Two sessions a day are offered. 305-451-1993.

Dolphin Research Center, US 1, Grassy Key (near Marathon Shores) is a nonprofit center offering educational tours Wednesday through Sunday. 305-289-1121 or 289-0002.

Theater of the Sea puts on a whale of a ninety-minute show featuring trained dolphins and sea lions, then invites visitors to ride the "bottomless" boat for a closer look at the friendly critters. Call ahead if you want to swim with the dolphins, a program that requires a half-hour orientation. 305-664-2431.

Dolphin Watch cruises aboard the Clearwater Ferry depart from the ferry station at the foot of Drew Street in downtown Clearwater three times a week to cruise St. Joseph Sound and the Gulf of Mexico. 813-442-7433.

Dolphin Watch cruises aboard Billy Graham's *Sea Pirate* sail at 10:00 A.M. on Saturdays from Shooter's in Melbourne for a four-hour cruise that includes an island barbecue; another boat sails at 1:00 P.M. on Wednesdays and Sundays for a two-and-a-half-hour lunch cruise. You're sure to see dolphins in the Intracoastal Waterway. 407-724-0024.

THE LOXAHATCHEE

Dense subdivisions crowd right up to the edge of the 145,000-acre **Loxahatchee National Wildlife Refuge**, located just west of the Florida Turnpike in southeastern Florida. Thousands of migrating birds winter in the teeming wetlands. On an airboat tour you'll see many natives, including the Everglades kite, the Florida sandhill crane, and more than your share of hungry alligators. Six miles west of US 441 on Lox Road, just north of Hillsboro Boulevard in Delray Beach. 407-734-8303. Open daily from 6:00 A.M. to 7:30 P.M. An admission fee is charged.

Loxahatchee Everglades Tours takes you on a high-speed airboat spin through the grassy glades. Naturalists serve as guides during the thirty- and forty-five-minute outings deep into a wilderness that is too wet for vehicles and too dry for boats.

Jonathan Dickinson State Park on the Loxahatchee River is named for a Quaker merchant who was shipwrecked near here while sailing from Port Royal, Jamaica, to Philadelphia 300 years ago. His party included his own family and slaves as well as a famous Quaker missionary of the times, Robert Barrow, and the ship's master. It's Dickinson's name that survives because the journal of his harrowing journey back to Philadelphia—during which he was pursued by Indians, hunger, and disease—became a seventeenth-century best-seller.

A more modern story concerns a loner known to his neighbors only as Trapper Nelson. He paddled up the Loxahatchee sometime around the 1920s and established a self-sufficient homestead. As civilization began to crowd in around him, he at first tried to accommodate it by charging admission to a primitive zoo he established on his land. However, as the pressures of modern zoning and taxation became more severe, he withdrew from public sight and closed his land to outsiders. In the 1960s he was found dead of a shotgun wound. His death was officially ruled a suicide but is still a mystery in some minds.

Aboard the thirty-passenger pontoon boat *Loxahatchee Queen*, with a park ranger as guide, visitors wind up the jungle-lined Loxahatchee to the old Trapper Nelson homestead. Now a state interpretive site, the homestead is preserved to

show the Florida subsistence lifestyle earlier in this century. Along the route you'll see stands of sand pine, pockets of mangrove swamp, alligators, osprey, and a wealth of wildlife. The Loxahatchee is a designated State Wild and Scenic River.

The park is located on US 1, twelve miles south of Stuart. 407-546-2771. Fees for boat tours are in addition to standard state park entry fees.

THE ST. JOHNS RIVER

Adventures in Florida offers tailor-made river cruises and airboat adventures that emphasize nature or history. Call for schedules, and ask about being picked up at your Orlando-land hotel. Lake Fairy Marina, Longwood. 407-331-0991.

Day Tripper Charters offers full- and half-day guided trips out of Sanford down the St. Johns River. The river here widens into huge Lake Monroe and wanders off into some of the system's most interesting and narrow waterways. Sanford Boat Works, Sanford. 407-330-1613.

Based in Florida's lake country, **Florida Seaplanes Inc.** can whisk you to Cape Canaveral to watch a launch, fly you over Cinderella's

Castle, or land you in one lake after another. It's a unique water experience, especially if you're interested in an overall view of the immense and complex St. Johns River system. It's also a unique flying adventure. Tours range in length from twenty minutes to one a half hours and require at least two passengers.

Planes are based in Sanford and other nearby lakes, so call for information and reservations. 904-343-2024, or 407-331-5155, or 407-846-3878.

Highbanks Marina in historic DeBary offers two-hour eco-tours of the St. Johns each Saturday afternoon. Campsites are also available at the marina, and camper guests get a discount on the cruise. Highbanks Marina, DeBary. 904-668-4491.

Hontoon Island Marina Eco-Tours are two-hour excursions through a narrow, tree-lined neck of the St. Johns near DeLand. Hontoon Island in the river here has been a landmark since earliest Indian times; a replica of an ancient totem that was found in the river can be seen on the island. A naturalist is on board to point out waterfowl, manatees, alligators, turtles, and much more.

Tours leave from the marina Tuesday,

Thursday, and Friday at 9:30 A.M. and stop at 10:15 A.M. at Blue Spring State Park for additional pickups. Hontoon Landing Resort and Marina, 2317 River Ridge Road, DeLand. 904-734-2474 or 800-248-2474.

On **St. Johns River Cruises and Tours**, the shallow-draft, clean, quiet, forty-eight-passenger *Native II* roams the most remote wilds of the St. Johns River Basin east of Lake Monroe through ancient bayous and worlds of wildlife. A Sanford native, Capt. Bob Hopkins narrates a nature cruise, pointing out wood stork and limpkin in the marshy shallows at the water's edge, seas of black-eyed Susans, entire islands aglow with wild hibiscus, and century-old cypresses that are the only survivors of a massive logging operation here earlier in this century. Fish feed among the cattails, and manatees come in winter to munch their way through tons of fragrant water hyacinths.

A lifelong river observer and nature lover, Hopkins knows every breeze and bayou of this little-traveled stretch of the St. Johns. An avid bird-watcher, he points out rare and endangered species and explains their most interesting points. During a two-hour sunset cruise, we saw several bald eagles, a couple of wild boars, a great blue heron with a freshly caught snake in its mouth, young alligators, and scores of leggy waterbirds stalking dinner along the shoreline.

Morning, afternoon, and sunset tours are offered, and from October through May, all-day tours are also available; call for reservations and instructions. Sanford is located off I-4 between Orlando and Daytona. *Native II* docks at the Osteen Bridge. 407-330-1612.

Airboat Rides through the headwaters of the St. Johns are offered by Linday's Fish Camp, 4650 East State 46, Geneva, 407-349-9726. Airboats also fly over the St. Johns out of State 50 in Christmas, Florida. 407-568-4307.

The **Dora Canal** is one of those "insider" Florida cruises that most visitors miss. A natural canal between lakes Dora and Eustis was widened during the steamboat era to make room for commercial traffic. The arrival of the railroads put an end to that, and the waterway was forgotten for generations. Now Captain Charlie takes visitors on one-and-a-half-hour cruises through one of the state's last remaining stands of virgin cypress forest. The swampy woods swarm with

wildlife: raccoons, alligators, wading birds, and turtles pick spots to doze in the sun.

Captain Charlie's Sightseeing Boat Cruises depart at 10:00 A.M. and 1:00 and 3:00 P.M. daily from Gator Inlet Marina on US 441 in Tavares. 904-343-0200.

Narrated tours of the canal are also offered by **Heritage Lake Tours**, Lake County Marina, US 441 west of the Dead River Bridge in Tavares. 904-343-4337.

Early Indians once lived the high life on the rich proteins supplied at **Tomoka State Park** by the waters of the Halifax and Tomoka rivers. Fish and shellfish were harvested from the warm, life-filled waters; wild roots and berries grew year-round along the mucky banks.

Aboard the little excursion boat operated by the state park, you'll cruise past old plantation sites where sugar planters had lavish mansions before they were burned out during the Seminole wars. A park ranger narrates the history and natural history.

The park, located at 2099 North Beach Street, Ormond Beach, 904-676-4050, also offers camping, nature trails, fishing, picnicking, canoeing, and a museum housing the paintings and sculptures of Fred Dana Marsh.

TURTLE WATCH

Loggerhead turtles, a threatened species, and endangered Green Leatherback sea turtles are chief among the armies of turtles that come ashore on Florida beaches on summer nights to lay their eggs by moonlight. The sight is unforgettable. Although turtles and their eggs are zealously protected, qualified naturalists do take small groups out to watch the egg laying phenomenon. Don't venture out alone at night in nesting areas. You could damage fragile nests and, in some cases, get arrested for trespassing (or worse). Poachers pay five-figure fines.

Turtle walks are available through many organizations, including these:

Florida Power and Light Company, Hutchinson Island. 800-552-8440.

Jensen Beach Chamber of Commerce. 407-334-3444.

Blowing Rocks Preserve, Jupiter Island. 407-575-2297.

Hobe Sound Nature Center, Hobe Sound. 407-546-2067.

Jupiter Beach Resort. 407-746-2511. Ask about packages that include accommodations, turtle walks, and other activities.

Gamble Rogers Memorial State Recreation Area, Flagler Beach. 904-439-2474.

SILVER SPRINGS

Far longer than man has lived in Florida, these massive springs have been spilling 823 cubic feet of sweet, 73-degree water into crystal clear pools every second of every day. It's the greatest spring in Florida and one of the greatest in the world. Its bounties were known to earliest Indians; its beauties weren't lost on Florida's first entrepreneurs. As early as 1898, visitors were touring the springs in glass-bottom rowboats.

Today Silver Springs is in transition from a major theme park to a state park. Take the nature cruise through thick jungle that's alive with native and exotic animals. The glass-bottom boat trips still glide over the spring "boil" just as they did nearly 100 years ago.

From I-75, take exit 69 and go east on State 40. 5656 East Silver Springs Boulevard, Ocala; 800-274-7458 or 904-236-1732.

Cruises of **Spruce Creek Environmental Preserve** are offered only once a month, but they're well worth all the planning it takes to schedule a boarding. The first shock is to pull off a major highway in highly populated Daytona Beach into a pristine, 150-acre wilderness by a cluster of buildings that are frozen in the 1930s.

The story is a fascinating one. James Gamble, of Proctor and Gamble fame, came up Spruce Creek in the 1890s. He liked the primeval jungle look of the land, so he bought 150 acres for a private hunting retreat. He built a "bungalow" (many of us would call it a small mansion) around 1907, and he soon added an orange-packing house for shipping citrus to his friends. In time, the estate grew to the impressive cluster of buildings that it is today.

One of the estate's most unusual features is the Snow White Cottage, built in 1938 in the "dark forest" style seen in the Walt Disney movie released that year. The fantasy landscape also includes a witch's hut, built from a 1,000-year-old cypress tree, and the Dwarf's Mineshaft (actually a children's playhouse) patterned after the one in the movie.

You'll also find a rustic gazebo, gardens, a hardwood forest that has changed little since Gamble first saw it a century ago, and other natural wonders. The greatest wonder of all, though, is Spruce Creek in all its pristine, jungle-trimmed beauty.

Gamble once navigated his sizable yacht up this creek (although to do so he had to have a railroad bridge taken down and reassembled—much to the delight of locals—every time he brought his yacht upstream). Since Gamble died in 1932, however, the creek in this area has been all but forgotten.

The preserve is operated by the Daytona Beach Museum of Arts and Sciences; you can gain access only through the museum. To tour the complex or to take the monthly cruise, call the museum at 904-255-0285.

At **Wakulla Springs State Park** you'll have a chance to cruise the largest and deepest freshwater spring in the world through a wilderness filled with sleepy alligators, darting shorebirds, sunning turtles, and leaping fish. The nature cruise, sometimes offered in a conventional boat and sometimes in a glass-bottom vessel, is one of the state's best. The park also offers swimming and snorkeling in a designated area (don't venture elsewhere because of the 'gators), picnicking, hiking among some of the state's largest hardwoods, and a rustic lodge with spacious rooms, marble baths, and an old-fashioned dining room serving hearty, down-home meals. Try the famous bean soup. For dining or room reservations at the lodge, call 904-224-5950. Wakulla Springs, south of Tallahassee; 904-222-7279.

THE LAW

It is against Florida state law to leave an animal in a vehicle. In the bright sun, temperatures build up quickly inside, even on cool days. Most major attractions have kennels where pets should be left.

5 Best of the Beaches

Florida's beaches are like fine wines. They are all good, but they range from mellow older vintages to bright bruts and sassy sparklers. To visit one beach is to take a mere sip. To become a true connoisseur of Florida beaches, you must know what beach goes with each mood, season, companion, or sport.

Some warnings are in order. If you want to swim in the ocean, with pulsing wave action and a limitless view of the Gulf or Atlantic, check a map before booking a hotel. Many fine resorts are actually located on bays or sounds. They may have good beaches, but they're not on the ocean. Others, especially in the Keys, are on the sea but don't have the sugar sand beaches Florida is famed for.

We've listed beaches by specialty.

BEST-KEPT SECRETS

If you like beaches off the beaten tourist track, try one of these: **Vilano Beach**, north of St. Augustine Beach but requiring the use of a different bridge; **Ponte Vedra Beach**, a public beach north of St. Augustine but hard to find because the exclusive community here does everything possible to discourage the hoi polloi;

Cumberland Island National Seashore, which is reached by ferry from St. Marys, Georgia; and **Pass-a-Grille** beach at the extreme south end of St. Petersburg Beach.

BICYCLING

The hard sands of most of the beaches from Daytona northward, including **Amelia Island** and **Jacksonville Beach**, are firm enough for bike riding. Some areas are also designated for automobile access. Salt water is extremely corrosive, however, so if you do ride on the beach, give the bicycle a thorough hosing and oiling afterward. You'll find bicycle rental agencies in every beach community; bicycles are provided free, or at modest cost, at some oceanfront resorts.

BIRD-WATCHING

Bird-watching is sublime at every Florida beach on our list, but it's especially busy and varied at the beaches at **Fort Pierce Inlet State Recreation Area**, any of the beaches along the **Merritt Island National Wildlife Refuge** (which lies under the Atlantic flyway), and at the beaches in **St. Joseph Peninsula State Park**, Port St. Joe, where 209 species have been logged. Other good birding beaches include **Anastasia Island, Bahia Honda, Big and Little Talbot islands, Caladesi Island, Cayo Costa, Fort Clinch/Amelia Island, Honeymoon Island, John D. MacArthur State Park, Long Key, St. Andrews Island, St. George Island, St. Joseph Peninsula, Sebastian Inlet, Wakulla Springs,** and **Wekiwa Springs.**

Audubon Island, a spoil bank in St. Andrews Bay in the Panhandle, is the only place between Mobile Bay and Cedar Key where brown pelicans breed and nest. A wilderness preserve to be enjoyed as you pass by on a boat (don't land here unless you're on an authorized expedition through the Audubon Society), it is also colonized by black skimmers and laughing gulls.

BOARDWALKS

Many Florida beaches have boardwalks for easier walking over fragile dunes, but when you want a

Boardwalk with a capital B, it's hard to beat **Daytona**'s strip of shops, vendors, arcades, miniature golf, and amusement rides. It's on the stretch of beach between Main and Ora streets. Nearby is the historic (1920s) band shell where frequent programs and concerts are held. **Panama City Beach** is even more commercial, with miles of amusements, T-shirt shops, and places to eat, drink, or be merry.

CAMPING

If you like beachside camping on white sand beaches, try the **St. Andrews State Recreation Area** near Panama City; 904-233-5140. Coastal camping is available at state parks such as **Grayton Beach**, 904-231-4210; **Cayo Costa**, 813-964-0375; **Fort Clinch**, 904-261-4212; **Gamble Rogers** (Flagler Beach), 904-439-2474; **Koreshan**, 813-992-0311; **Little Talbot Island**, 904-251-2300; **St. Andrews**, 904-233-5140; **St. George Island**, 904-927-2111; **St. Joseph Peninsula**, 904-227-1327; and **Sebastian Inlet**, 407-546-2771.

DISABILITIES

"Pathways to the Sea" allow the physically challenged person easier access to the beach at **Crandon Park** on Key Biscayne, Miami. The drive-on beaches of the **Daytona** area are also a good choice because the car can drive onto the beach and the wheelchair can operate on the sand.

Again, be aware that a wheelchair will need a thorough cleaning after contact with salt water.

FINE SANDS

The beaches of the Panhandle, most notably those from Panama City to Pensacola, are a uniquely fine, white silica sand that crunches under foot much like new-fallen snow. In fact, we've seen children skiing down the dunes (a practice that is discouraged because of the fragility of the dunes and sea oats). No one can dispute that the most blindingly beautiful beaches in the state are those along the Gulf in this area. This is four-season Florida, so it can be much hotter in summer than the rest of the peninsula, and it's subject to cold snaps in winter.

Among the best of these beaches are those at **Perdido Key State Recreation Area** fifteen miles southwest of Pensacola, **Henderson Beach State Recreation Area** just east of Destin, and **Grayton Beach State Recreation Area** on County 30A south of US 98 between Fort Walton Beach and Panama City.

Most beaches on the east and west coasts of the state have granular, brown-sugar sand. The beaches of southwest Florida (Sanibel, Marco) are often composed of shell rubble that makes barefoot walking difficult but shell collecting very good.

HISTORY

A doubloon could wash ashore almost anywhere, but some of the best beaches for history buffs include the following:

Canaveral National Seashore deserves listing in many of the "best of" areas here, but of special interest to history fanciers are Turtle Mound, an archaeological site with shell mounds built by pre-Columbian Indians; and the ghost town of Eldora, a community that was built here before the turn of the century. The twenty-four-mile-long seashore is on State A1A about seven miles south of New Smyrna Beach. The visitors center offers a slide program. 904-428-3384.

Cape Florida State Recreation Area is now recovered from Hurricane Andrew, but it took the full fury of the storm. As tragic as they are in human terms, hurricanes reshape Florida beaches and berms and make them more beautiful. The beach here is sensational, but it's the lighthouse that makes this a fascinating historical footnote as well.

Built in 1825, the Cape Florida Light was attacked during the Seminole wars. Trapped high in the lighthouse when the Indians started to set it afire, the lighthouse keeper and his assistant tried one last, desperate ploy. They rolled a keg of gunpowder down the 122 steps, setting off an explosion that routed the Indians and alerted a boat offshore to come to their rescue. The park is on the southern tip of Key Biscayne, which is reached from Miami via the Rickenbacker Causeway.

Fort Zachary Taylor State Historic Site in

Key West dates to 1845, shortly after Florida became a state. It's named for President Taylor, who died in office early in the year construction began on the fort. There's a swimming beach, picnic facilities, showers, and snacks. 305-292-6713.

Gulf Islands National Seashore at Pensacola Beach has miles of magnificent sand beaches in the shadow of Fort Pickens, an enormous brick fort where Apache warrior Geronimo was imprisoned. Also located here is Fort Barrancas. Both forts can be toured for free. 904-934-2600. As you walk the beaches in this area in the shimmery heat of a hot day, you can almost see the Spanish soldiers who, with 100 Aztec warriors, arrived here in galleons in 1559. A ship thought to have been one of that fleet was found off Emanuel Point in 1993 and it is being studied by archaeologists.

On **Hutchinson Island**, strands of sand punctuated by bold rocks form a picturesque beach where you'll find the last House of Refuge. Once, these rescue stations could be found along the entire coast. It was near here in 1696 that Jonathan Dickinson and his family were shipwrecked while sailing home from Jamaica.

They were captured by Indians, tortured, and starved. Dickinson's journal, which is still in print, tells the story of his family's escape and return to the safety of the Northeast. Dickinson eventually became mayor of Philadelphia. The House of Refuge is open daily except Monday and holidays. A small admission fee is charged. 407-225-1875.

Jacksonville Beach still uses as a lifeguard station one of the oldest Red Cross Stations on the east coast. You'll find it where Beach Boulevard (US 90) meets the ocean.

St. Andrews State Park in the Panhandle is a beachgoer's dream come true. Its quartz beaches and windblown dunes are breathtaking. Its emerald waters are clear as a gemstone, its facilities are good (picnic tables, rest rooms), its nature trails run with deer and birdlife, and it has a historic plus. Here you'll find a reconstructed Cracker Turpentine Still. Once covered with pine forests, much of northern Florida has always been an important source of naval stores, including turpentine.

Southernmost Beach in Key West calls itself the farthest south beach in the United States. In any case, every point in Key West is only a few footsteps away from an ancient fort or another historic point of interest.

HORSEBACK RIDING

Splashing through the surf line on horseback is a heady and unique way to enjoy Florida beaches. At Amelia Island, guided rides are available from **Seahorse Stables**. 904-261-4878.

SHELLING

The biggest and most colorful seashells are rarely found along pounding surf lines. Look for them on quiet backwater beaches where stranded shells are gently nudged ashore and washed clean. Once the shelling mecca of the state, Sanibel has become so popular that serious shell seekers start their beachcombing at first light. The surest way to find shells is to take a day cruise to an offshore island or sandbar. Skippers often choose the day's destination after determining where winds and tides have been most likely to create the best shelling. For information call the Lee County Convention and Visitors Bureau, 800-533-4753. Good shelling beaches include the following.

Delnor-Wiggins Pass State Recreation Area is a windblown sandspit at the outlet of the Cocohatchee River into the Gulf of Mexico. To the east lie mangrove swamps; the beach is lined with dunes and a frieze of cabbage palms. On summer nights, turtles come ashore to lay their eggs. 11100 Gulf Shore Boulevard North, Naples. 813-597-6196.

Don Pedro Island State Recreation Area is a barrier island between Knight Island and Little Gasparilla west of Fort Myers. For ferry information, call 813-964-0375.

Gasparilla Island State Recreation Area was once the home of pirate Jose Gaspar. Shelling is especially good here after westerly winds in winter. It's reached via a toll causeway at County 775 and Placida, Boca Grande. 813-964-0375.

John D. MacArthur Beach State Park, on a barrier island in north Palm Beach County, is one of the few places along the wave-pounded open Atlantic seashore where shelling is good. The beach is wide, clean, and sandy, and the stands of tropical and subtropical trees provide habitat for a host of rare and endangered wildlife.

*Search the
backwater beaches
for shells*

It's located 2.8 miles south of the corner of US 1 and PGA Boulevard.

Shell Island, off Panama City Beach, is an uninhabited sandspit in the process of becoming a state park. Almost a mile wide and nearly eight miles long, the white-sugar beach here is a good place to look for shells. It's accessible only by boat, but a half dozen boats out of Panama City Beach offer various passages to the island.

Siesta Key near Sarasota is not just a good shelling beach, it was named by a major travel magazine as one of the three best beaches in the entire *world*.

'Tween Waters Inn, Captiva Island, offers shelling cruises. 813-472-1015.

Sea Excursions out of Marco Island takes shellers to Cape Romano, Keeywadin Island, or Tigertail or Hideaway beaches, preferably on a low tide after a westerly storm. 813-642-6400.

SNORKELING

Snorkeling in Florida's springs can be cold, but the waters are always clear. In the ocean, stormy weather can stir up silt in the waters, clouding them for the snorkeler. The calm weather of

---

THE BEST STATE PARKS*
FOR SNORKELING

Bahia Honda	Peacock Springs
Blue Spring	Pennekamp Coral Reef
DeLeon Springs	San Pedro
Ichetucknee Springs	St. Andrews
John D. MacArthur	St. Joseph Peninsula
John U. Lloyd	St. Lucie Inlet
Long Key	Wekiwa Springs
Manatee Springs	

*For a brochure listing all state park addresses, phone numbers, and facilities, write Florida Tourism, 126 West Van Buren Street, Tallahassee, FL 32399.

---

summer is best for snorkeling ocean reefs, but don't ever pass up a chance to put on flippers and mask and open a window on the fascinating undersea world of freshwater Florida too.

SPRING BREAK

The 1960 film *Where the Boys Are* brought students to Fort Lauderdale beaches by the carload, and other cities wanted to get on the bandwagon. However, with the kids came drug overdosing, falls from hotel balconies, drunk-driving arrests, and, in general, an image that towns like Fort Lauderdale and Daytona decided they no longer wanted to project. Advertising slants changed; spring break activities were discontinued or curtailed.

If you're looking this year for where the boys are, get the latest buzz, because spring break could be anywhere or nowhere in the Sunshine State.

SPRINGS

Some of the largest sweetwater springs in the United States are found in Florida. DeLeon Springs is thought to have been Ponce de Leon's original Fountain of Youth. Blue Spring is among the springs where manatee take refuge in cold weather. Crystal Springs bubble up into the Gulf of Mexico, providing a freshwater cocktail where divers and manatee play together. The springs stay 68–72 degrees winter and summer, providing a warm swim in winter and a refreshing cooldown in summer.

Below we list some of the state's best springs for swimming, most of them pristine waters from the same aquifer that provides much of the state's drinking water supply.

DeLeon Springs State Recreation Area has a deep, spacious swimming area, grassy green grounds, and a rustic restaurant where you can order whole-grain batters and cook your own pancakes. The site of an old Spanish sugar mill, it's thought by some to be Ponce de Leon's Fountain of Youth. It is west of Daytona Beach, north of DeLand. 904-985-4212.

At **Ichetucknee Springs State Park**, 233 million gallons of crystal water spew out of the ground and create the Ichetucknee River, which in turn flows into the Santa Fe. In an inner tube or raft, you can float the spring run through mossy glades and live oak forests. Call ahead for information about renting equipment and riding the free shuttle that takes "tubers" back to the parking lot. The park is northeast of Fort White off State 47 and 238. 904-497-2511.

Manatee Springs State Park will remind you of the ol' swimmin' hole of your youth. Bracing waters spill from the ground, form a swimming pool, then flow off through a cypress and sweetgum forest on their way to the Suwannee River. The park is at the end of State 320 off US 98, six miles west of Chiefland. 904-493-6072.

Peacock Springs State Recreation Area, Luraville, sixteen miles southeast of Live Oak on State 51. 904-497-2511.

At **Wekiwa Springs State Park** you can swim in the springs or canoe the spring run. It's northwest of Orlando in Altamonte (pronounced "alta-mont") Springs on State 436. 407-884-2009.

SPUME AND SURF

It's not a swimming beach, but the bold, rocky coast opposite **Washington Oaks State Park**, two miles south of St. Augustine on State A1A, forms one of the state's loveliest, most bouldery seascapes. As the tide recedes, pools remain in the sculptured coquina rocks, forming a smorgasbord for shorebirds who come to dine on stranded fish and shells. The rock sculptures at **Blowing Rock State Preserve** on Jupiter Island, off Hobe Sound, are so large that the surf is sometimes turned into big geysers as it crashes through blowholes.

SURFING

You'll see surfboards and boogie boards anywhere along Florida's Atlantic coast, especially when winds have kicked up the combers, but the best surfing is generally found between **Sebastian Inlet** and **Cocoa Beach**. Try the **Monster Hole** next to the south jetty at Sebastian Inlet, the shores off **Patrick Air Force Base**, **Indian River Lagoon**, and the town of **Indialantic**. For more information, call the Cocoa Beach Tourism Council at 407-459-2200.

Also known for surfing is the fine family beach at **Fort Pierce Inlet State Recreation Area** on the south end of North Hutchinson Island, and **Sebastian Inlet State Recreation Area** north of Vero Beach. In south Florida, the best bets are the **First Street Beach** in Miami Beach and **South Beach Park** in Boca Raton. Some people surf at **Jacksonville Beach**.

The next best thing to real surf, and a lot

more dependable, are the huge waves at **Typhoon Lagoon** at Walt Disney World. One ticket price buys all-day admission to all the lagoon's rides, reefs, pools, and slides.

TOPLESS SUNNING

Unofficially speaking, hangouts for nude sunbathers include **Playalinda Beach** on the Space Coast, **Virginia Beach** on Virginia Key (off the Rickenbacker Causeway in Miami), **Beer Can Island** off Davis Island in Tampa Bay, and the more remote reaches of **Egmont Key** at the entrance to Tampa Bay. However, our advice is to observe and follow local custom because city fathers anywhere in the state occasionally get tough on alternative bathing costumes. Topless sunning is seen commonly in **Key West**, with its maverick spirit and many European visitors. Other communities, by contrast, have elaborately written anatomical descriptions of just how much skin a bather can show before he or she is hauled off to the judge.

TROPICAL BEAUTY

If you want the shade of lush, tropical trees and foliage in addition to sunny sands, here are some of the best beaches:

Bahia Honda State Park has some of the most rare and beautiful, truly tropical vegetation in the state. Here you'll find not just dazzling sand beaches on both Florida Bay and the Atlantic, but mangrove forests, dunes, and hardwood hammocks. Caribbean trees such as the yellow satinwood, poisonous manchineel, and key thatch palm are seen here. Among the rare plants found here is the small flowered lily thorn. The park is on Big Pine Key south of Marathon. 305-872-2353.

Delnor-Wiggins Pass State Recreation Area is a natural barrier island blessed with stands of sea grape and cabbage palms, dunes peppered with sea oats, and a backdrop of mangrove trees with their roots in salt water. A long, shallow beach is right on the Gulf of Mexico. South of Bonita Springs, take US 41 and go west on County 901. 813-597-6196.

John U. Lloyd Beach State Recreation Area is one of the Fort Lauderdale area's best-

Some of Florida's beaches offer lush foliage as well as sunny sands

LEAVE LIVE CREATURES BEHIND

There are two good reasons not to take *live* sea-shells, starfish, and other sea creatures. The first is environmental. They're part of nature's scheme and should be left alone. The second is practical. The cleaning process for live or newly deceased mollusks is at best unpleasant. At its worst, dead tissue ruins luggage and clothing, makes people sick from the smell, and attracts flies and ants.

Any shell, no matter how old, may contain tissue. Long after the original animal left, a hermit crab could have moved in. Boiling water, chlorine bleach, and sometimes alcohol are used to clean shells. You can soak sand dollars, one of the most popular and common catches on the Florida coast, briefly in a mild bleach solution and then coat them with a glaze made from Elmer's glue diluted with water.

A helpful guidebook to shell preparation and crafts is *Beachcombing and Beachcrafting* by Anne Westcott Dodd (Wescott Cove Publishing Company). The best pocket identification guide is *Seashells of North America* by R. Tucker Abbott (Golden Press).

kept secrets. You can see it from Port Everglades, but to reach it you have to go south to Dania on US 1 and then double back on a long spit of land until you're almost back where you started at Port Everglades. Backing the broad, brown-sugar beach is a thick forest of casuarina trees, known as "singing pines." Picnic in their cool shade and listen to their song when the wind blows through them.

Long Key State Recreation Area, with its tropical hammock growths, such as sea grape, gumbo-limbo trees, mahogany, and crabwood, also has good swimming in shallow, warm waters. It's at Mile Marker 67.5, Florida Keys.

THE BEACHES OF WALT DISNEY WORLD

Only Disney could create such magic in what was once Florida swamp and savannah. Exquisite white sand beaches rim lakes at the Polynesian, Grand Floridian, and Yacht and Beach Club resorts. Fort Wilderness, WDW's campground, also has a magnificent beach. Water theme parks in WDW are Typhoon Lagoon and River Country.

North Shore State Recreation Area, a forty-acre park, is an unspoiled tropical Eden with a sandy strand rimmed by heavy jungle in the shadow of Miami Beach's high-rise hotels. It's east of Collins Avenue between 79th and 87th streets.

ABOUT SCUBA DIVING

There is no major coastal city in Florida where scuba training, equipment, and excursions are not available. Almost any sizable resort can book a dive for you, and many resorts also offer basic scuba training in their swimming pools.

Rather than listing the best reefs and wrecks, we suggest that you connect at your destination with a qualified dive charter operator who can take you diving in the area that is best for your abilities and for the day's sea conditions. Although people have written entire books about the state's best scuba spots, most of them assume that you have your own boat. If you will be relying on guides, outfitters, and scuba boat skippers, we offer a few suggestions.

Outfitters in the Keys include **Silent World Dive Center** in Key Largo, 305-451-3252 or 800-966-DIVE; **Conch Republic Divers**, MM 90.3, 305-852-1655; **Aquasphere Diving**, Islamorada, 305-664-2833 or 800-362-4957; **Bud and Mary's**, Islamorada, 305-664-2211 or 800-344-7352; **Floridaze Dive Center**, 305-852-1432 or 800-437-3483; and **Tavernier Dive Center**, 305-664-9312 or 800-245-DIVE.

Key West has two main reefs. Snorklers and novice divers prefer the shallow, inner reef. The outer reef, which is deeper, has larger sea life and more wrecks, and between the two is an intermediate reef. **ViewFinder Dive Center** in the Overseas Market Mall in Key West offers dive trips on boats that were designed from the keel up as dive boats. Two-tank, two-location trips leave daily at 9:00 A.M. and 1:30 P.M. Shallower reef dives are also offered. Special trips include a three-tank dive trip to the Marquesas and a four-tank dive trip to the Dry Tortugas. One- to eight-day scuba classes, from the introductory to the professional level, are also available.

Reefs at Looe Key Marine Sanctuary are as spectacular as those of the better-known Pennekamp Reef off Key Largo. It's off Ramrod Key. One outfitter is **Looe Key Dive Center**; 800-942-5397.

In the Palm Beaches, contact **South Florida Diving Headquarters**, 800-258-3483 or 800-258-DIVE.

In the Panhandle, get in touch with **Hydrospace Dive Shop**, Panama City Beach, 904-234-9463; **Panama City Dive Center**, 904-235-3390 or 800-832-DIVE; **Diver's Den**, 904-234-8717.

To dive the reefs and wrecks off Marco Island, contact **Aqua Adventures**, 813-394-DIVE. Two-tank half-day boat dives are offered complete with dive master, optional videotaping, and equipment if you need it.

Contact the **Florida Association of Dive Shop Operators**, 335 Beard Street, Tallahassee, FL 32303 for a current list of outfitters and guides.

CAVE AND CAVERN DIVING

Also popular are dives deep into the caves that surround the state's many springs (where permitted). Cave and cavern diving are, however, specialties that divers should not attempt without specific training. One source of cave diving courses is **Branford Dive Center**, US 27 at the Suwannee River in Branford; 904-935-1141 or 935-0146. Also write the **National Association for Cave Diving**, Box 14492, Gainesville, FL 32604.

Wreck diving is another specialty that requires additional training and safety equipment. Note that snorkeling is allowed almost anywhere that swimming is permitted; scuba diving is not.

The following areas are good places for cave diving.

Ginnie Springs near the community of High Springs has a guideline that leads divers to a depth of sixty feet into the Cathedral, which is seventy-eight feet long and seventy-two feet wide with a ceiling thirty-eight feet high.

Branford-Suwannee has a number of caves. Get training and directions from the Branford Dive Center (see above).

Blue Grotto, near Williston, is a natural sinkhole that can be dived to a depth of about 100 feet.

Crystal River is fed by many springs, including Kings Spring, Mullet Spring, and Grand Canyon Spring. Many of the springs have underwater caverns that divers like to explore.

If you're a diver and want to experience one

of scuba's most thrilling and unusual overnight stays, check into **Jules Undersea Lodge**, which lies five fathoms under the surface just next to Pennekamp Coral Reef State Park. Accommodations include a galley with provisions, entertainment electronics, bathrooms, and big windows that look out into the reef world. Swim down, enter the living area to spend the night in comfort, then don your gear to surface again. 305-451-2353.

THE SUM OF THE BEACH

A modest admission fee, usually a few dollars per carload, is charged to enter Florida state parks, state recreation areas, and many city, county, and national beach sites. Beach ramp tolls apply at Daytona Beach if you drive onto the beach. Beachfronts in highly populated areas may have metered parking.

WHAT'S IN A NAME?

Nicknames can be a mixed blessing. Some are applied to enhance the image of a destination. Others are used to refer collectively to a long string of islands or communities that want to market themselves as a group. Florida watchers find the coining of nicknames amusing; tourists can find it confusing if not downright infuriating. Below we list some of the official and slang terms that are applied to various Florida beaches.

Calling themselves the **Conch Republic**, the Keys seceded from the United States a few years ago after roadblocks were set up on US 1 to search for drugs. (Key West natives are known as Conchs—it rhymes with "bonks.") Conchs have come back into the fold, but they still consider themselves a republic apart. Happy visitors agree that the Keys are an American Riviera different from anywhere else in the state.

Gold Coast traditionally means Miami, with other south Florida communities going along for the ride, depending on how closely they want to be identified with Miami.

Discovery Coast refers to the St. Augustine area.

First Coast refers to the Jacksonville–St. Augustine area.

ABOUT WATER HAZARDS

Attacks by sharks and barracuda have occurred in the waters surrounding Florida, and every few years there is a tragedy involving an alligator on a lake or river, but these incidents are always publicized out of proportion. Greater dangers to swimmers include run-outs or rip-tides, and stings from the Portuguese man-o-war, a type of jellyfish. Both hazards are rare, and they are present only during certain wind and current conditions. It's best to swim near lifeguard stations, where you can get current information and warnings. Lifeguards are trained not only in rescue techniques but in first aid for the kinds of stings and injuries you're most likely to encounter.

By far, the biggest danger to Florida beachgoers is sunburn. The following tips were put together by lifeguards, suntan lotion manufacturers, and Daytona Beach tourism personnel:

Day 1: Use Sun Protection Factor (SPF) 15 or higher everywhere skin is exposed. Don't forget your face.

Day 2: Continue with the same SPF.

Day 3: If you started with an SPF higher than 15, drop to 15 today. If you started with 15, use it for one more day.

Day 4: Move down the SPF ladder. If your skin is fair, stay with SPF 15. If it's fair to medium, drop to SPF 10; if it's tan to olive, try SPF 8 or 6; if it's deep to dark, use SPF 4. Use a higher SPF on your face to avoid wrinkling.

Day 5 and beyond: Continue as on Day 4.

Added tip: Keep your skin protectors in your drink cooler.

To this we add a few more advisories:

Reapply protective lotions as often as necessary after swimming or sweating.

Drink plenty of water and make sure that small children who can't ask for a drink also get plenty of water.

When snorkeling in Florida's very clear waters, wear waterproof sun protectors and a light garment, such as pajamas, that covers the arms and legs. Without realizing it, you can get a very bad burn through the water.

When driving home from a day at the beach, remember that prolonged brightness may affect your night vision. Wear good sunglasses by day; try to get home before dark.

Summertime is stingray season. Nestling in the sand in warm, shallow water, rays won't lash out at you without provocation but, if stepped on, will instinctively stab out with a barbed tail. Don't stamp and splash through the water; instead just shuffle along. If you do bumble into a ray, it will probably dart away.

Emerald Coast is the Panhandle, with its jade waters and incredibly white sand.

Lee Island Coast is a clever play on words. On the leeward side of the state, Lee County is the home of Fort Myers, laying claim too to Charlotte County and all the wonderful islands up and down this coastline.

The Palm Beaches include the very exclusive island communities of Palm Beach County, the huge metropolis that is West Palm Beach, and parts of the Everglades stretching to Lake Okeechobee.

10,000 Islands is an island-pocked portion of the Everglades from Marco Island southward.

Space Coast is the Cape Canaveral area.

Suncoast is used to refer to communities in the St. Petersburg area.

Treasure Coast generally refers to the Fort Pierce–Stuart area.

DON'T PICK THE SEA OATS

Sea oats form an important network that keeps sands in place. It is against the law to pick or disturb them.

SWIMMING WITH DOLPHINS

For a price, you can swim briefly with the dolphins at Dolphins Plus, Key Largo, 305-451-1993; Theater of the Sea in Islamorada, 305-664-2431; and the Dolphin Research Center in Marathon, 305-289-1121. A dolphin program is available to guests only at Hawk's Cay Resort, 305-743-6000.

Many marine theme parks have dolphin petting tanks; at Marineland, visitors are invited to feed leaping dolphins, which snatch fish from the hand. Programs in which dolphins are confined are increasingly controversial in the state, so check ahead to see what programs are available during your visit.

AND THE WINNERS ARE . . .

When United States beaches were ranked by University of Maryland coastal geologist Stephen Leatherman according to forty points (including appearance, water quality, and temperature), five of the top ten were in Florida. And the winners are: Bahia Honda in the Keys, Grayton Beach and St. George Island in the Panhandle, Caladesi Island off Clearwater, and Crandon Park in Miami.

PITCH IN

Beach cleanups along Florida lakes and rivers are sponsored regularly by local and regional groups. If you want to help, it's best to contact a local group for information. Information about International Coastal Clean-Up Day is also available from the Center for Marine Conservation, Suite 500, 1725 DeSales Street N.W., Washington, D.C. 20036.

Driving the Coastal Highways

Florida doesn't offer the type of sweeping, sightseeing coastal highways found in Oregon and northern California. Driving coastal roads almost always means heavy local traffic, long delays for bridge openings, occasional backtracking where roads end at the sea, and frequent detours back to the mainland to get past wide inlets that are not bridged. For miles along many seaside roads, you can't see the sea because the view is solidly blocked by hotels or homes.

Great rivers cleave cities in two, and routes have to be planned according to where you can cross bridges. Tampa and St. Petersburg were once so many road miles apart that entrepreneurs

started an airline just to bridge them. The world's first scheduled flights used flying boats to carry one passenger at a time across Tampa Bay before World War I.

Without a good map, you will dead-end at the water time after time, especially in Fort Lauderdale with its miles of canals. With map in hand, consider taking some of the rides we list below.

THE PRETTIEST SEA HIGHWAYS

The Overseas Highway, which runs 100 awesome miles from Key Largo to Key West, is an engineering marvel that includes the famous Seven Mile Bridge. In spots it's like floating far out to sea, with nothing but water on both sides.

Addresses in the Keys are given in mile markers (for example, MM 45.6). MM 0 is in Key West; the road ends above Homestead at MM 127. Street names are used only in communities wide enough to have more than one road.

Pull off to enjoy the nature show, a picnic, quaint shops and restaurants, and fishing from abandoned bridges. Beaches are few; the best public beaches are at Bahia Honda, Long Key, and Key West. Good small beaches are found at Sombrero Beach (near MM 50) and Key Colony Beach, a community known for its strict enforcement of speed limits.

A good midway stop is The Rain Barrel at mile marker 86.7 in Islamorada. Artists from around the world work here in their own studios and gardens, offering their wares for sale.

The roadbed was originally a railroad that was destroyed in a deadly hurricane in the 1930s. A marker near Islamorada honors 425 passengers who died in a train in which they were trying to escape the Keys; the total death count throughout the islands will never be known. At Pigeon Key,

a 1908 railroad workers' camp is being restored as a nature center and rail museum.

If you're in a hurry to rush on through to Key West, don't drive. Fly. The Overseas Highway is only two lanes in spots, and it slows to a crawl in settlements when local traffic is heavy. Many cars are towing campers or boats, which makes them slow and cumbersome. You could be stuck behind one for miles before coming to a passing lane.

The Overseas Highway (US 1) is a drive to take at a leisurely pace, to savor and enjoy. Take as long as you can spare to try all there is to

---

KEY LIMES

True key lime pie is yellow, not green. Key limes are not at all like the familiar Persian limes available in supermarkets. They're small, round, yellow, and extremely juicy—a lime taste tinged with a hint of vanilla. Keys old-timers disagree on whether "real" key lime pie has a graham-cracker or a pastry crust and whether it's topped with meringue or whipped cream. Let them bicker, but try them all and decide for yourself.

offer. Snorkel the best reefs, take every side trip, try to spot some miniature Key deer, sidle up to a chickee bar each day at sundown, and stop at lots of restaurants to see who makes the best key lime pie.

For information on the Keys, call 800-FLA-KEYS.

The Sunshine Skyway Bridge closes the end of Tampa Bay, allowing drivers to go from St. Petersburg to Bradenton in mere minutes, a drive that once took hours. The view of the Bay to the east and the Gulf of Mexico to the west is spectacular. A toll is charged. The bridge is located on I-275 between St. Petersburg and Bradenton.

On the **Panhandle Coast**, the drive between Carrabelle and Panama City, passing through Apalachicola and dozens of villages that seem frozen in time, makes a pretty ride. Take State A1A from Eastpoint out onto St. George Island, and drive the long, narrow sandspit for ten miles out to sea. Jump off the main road again near Port St. Joe to drive out a sliver of sand on the St. Joseph Peninsula, where a state park offers picnic tables and campsites.

West of Panama City, take Alternate US 98, then County 30A to stay with the shoreline. The road eventually rejoins US 98. Santa Rosa Island, home of the Gulf Islands National Seashore, is a narrow corridor of granulated-sugar sands. You can reach it via toll bridges from Navarre or Gulf Breeze.

Perdido Key is more of the same, but to reach it you'll have to go back to the mainland, then south on State 297 and out to the hamlet of Gulf Beach on State 292. The road leads along the Gulf to the Perdido Key State Preserve and then across the Alabama state border.

The **Dunedin Causeway** takes you west off Alternate US 19 north of Dunedin to picture-pretty Honeymoon Island State Recreation Area. Walk trails through one of the last virgin stands of slash pine in the state, watching for osprey and cormorants. Swim from the white sand beach and then have a picnic.

Canaveral National Seashore, the Space Coast, covers thousands of acres of water, marsh, and beach, including twenty miles of some of the most beautiful swimming beaches in the state. It's along State A1A south of New Smyrna Beach. The road simply peters out and forms a path that can be traveled on bicycle or foot. Cars must backtrack, getting a double dose of the dazzling panorama of sand, sea, sunshine, and shorebirds.

LIVE OAKS AND SEASCAPES

Amelia Island isn't easy to find on a map, but it's the home of Fernandina Beach in far northeastern Florida. The beaches that rim the entire east side of the island are satiny, wave-washed sands so firm you can drive on them (where allowed). Or, take winding roads behind the high barrier dunes through forests of wind-warped live oaks. From Fernandina Beach, head north again out North Fletcher Avenue, following signs to Fort Clinch. The state park has marvelous beaches, campsites, picnicking, and a grand brick fort dating from the Seminole wars era. 800-2-AMELIA.

MAYPORT AND THE FERRY

Home of the naval air station, **Mayport** offers one of the state's most scenic routes and one of its best bargains. The Mayport ferry has been taking people and cars across the mouth of the St. Johns River for decades. Start your drive as far south as Vilano Beach opposite St. Augustine. Except for busy streets around Jacksonville Beach, you'll have open views for miles of frothy surf. The hazy Atlantic stretches as far as you can see, and lonely beaches are patrolled by soaring pelicans. At Mayport, take the car ferry (for a small fee) across to State 105. The ferry runs daily on the half hour from 6:30 A.M. to 10:00 P.M. Rustic and unpretentious Singleton's Seafood Shack is just the right place to have a fresh seafood meal while you watch enormous ships head out to sea. 904-798-9148.

Turn north on Fort George Island to visit Kingsley Plantation. Suddenly the bright beach world becomes a dark forest of stately live oaks leading to a plantation where slave baron Jeremiah Kingsley once lived. The house has been restored; you can still see remains of the original slave cabins. Once you're back on State A1A, go east to Little Talbot Island State Park, with its seaside views, campsites, five miles of beach, and picnic facilities.

VILLAGES BY THE SEA

Apalachicola started life as a cotton port but has made its fortune on the bountiful 10,000 acres of oyster beds that cluster offshore. The earliest Spanish explorers set up a shipbuilding center here in the sixteenth century, harvesting pine for masts and live oak for stout timbers from the dense upland forests that now make up the Apalachicola National Forest.

In early November, the community fills with tourists for an annual blessing of the fleet and seafood festival. The rest of the year it's a quiet backwater overlooking the bay. The Gibson Inn is a quaint old three-story hotel dating to 1907; Trinity Church was built in 1839 from prefabricated components that were shipped in from New York.

A small museum here honors Dr. John Gorrie, who, in desperation to cool his patients during yellow fever epidemics, invented the first ice-making machine. The original is in the Smithsonian. The museum is open Thursday through Monday except on major holidays.

Southwest of Tallahassee on US 98. For information, contact the Chamber of Commerce at 128 Market Street, Apalachicola, FL 32320; 904-653-9419.

Cedar Key is a sort of seaside Brigadoon on the Gulf coast. It appears to have slumbered in sun-baked silence for the entire century since its boomtown days. Reached from the mainland by a causeway that seems to take you out to sea and off the edge of the world, it's named for the cedar trees that once covered the land. They were harvested to the last splinter to use in making pencils.

The salt industry here was so important to food preservation during the Civil War that Cedar Key became a prize of war. Florida's first railroad had been opened in 1861 between Cedar Key and another boomtown, Fernandina Beach. Both were passed by as the need for larger, deeper harbors arose.

Today Cedar Key is a sleepy fishing village, popular with artists and laid-back vacationers who come for the ramshackle, salty, Old Florida ambience. Don't expect touristy whoop-de-do. Instead, settle for a breezy room overlooking the water, some fine little museums, and some of the best dining in the state. For information, call the Chamber of Commerce at 904-543-5600.

Nine miles east of the village on State 24, you'll find the 30,784-acre Waccasassa Bay State Preserve and the 4,000-acre Cedar Key Scrub State Preserve. Salt marsh threaded with tidal creeks and sprouting scrubby pine in higher spots, this area is the last remaining remnant of what was once a vast Gulf hammock. Observe the rich birdlife from your car, or hike the service roads. Hunting is permitted from September through December in the Cedar Key Scrub Preserve, so take appropriate precautions when hiking here. 904-543-5567.

Fernandina Beach, now a half-forgotten hamlet northeast of Jacksonville, was once one of Florida's richest cities. Adventurers poured in to exploit its harbor, dealing and dueling to the extent that the city has served under eight flags, including that of Mexico. Larger, deeper harbors and wider highways lured traffic away from Fernandina, leaving it with street after street of magnificent Victorian mansions. Residents held on, but there was no money to modernize the homes. As a result, entire Victorian neighborhoods remain authentic and intact. The downtown area is a streetscape of quaint shops and restaurants, shrimp boats, transient yachts, and the oldest saloon in the state, complete with swinging doors.

Take the State A1A (Yulee) exit east off I-95 north of Jacksonville. The road ends in Fernandina Beach. For information, call 800-2-AMELIA or write the Chamber of Commerce, 102 Centre Street, Fernandina Beach, FL 32034. The Chamber, housed in an old railroad depot at the head of Centre Street, is an excellent resource. Unfortunately, it's open only during weekday business hours.

Miami Beach is more like Manhattan with palm trees than it is a quaint village, but the area known as South Beach deserves mention because it's the largest neighborhood of Art Deco buildings in the world. It's a Mediterranean village without the hills, a smart and cosmopolitan collection of closely packed bistros, sidewalk cafés, clubs, and restaurants across the street from one of the state's widest and most beautiful brown sand beaches.

The area was developed intensely in the 1920s through the 1940s, in a garish Deco style that attracted the glitterati of the times but that soon became declassé. High-rise hotels were built farther north on Collins Avenue, directly on the beach. The hotels of South Beach became dreary residential hotels for the elderly. By the 1960s there was talk of bulldozing the entire mess.

Fortunately, a young and arty crowd was able to look at the Deco designs with fresh eyes and see that they were fine representations of a bygone era of neon lights, round windows, and ice cream colors. People began buying up and restoring the old warehouses and hotels and turning them into chic clubs, inns, and restaurants.

This is an area where you'll see Hasidic Jews in black bowlers and long black frock coats, European models posing against the world-famous Deco background, young honeymooners, sun-burned Brits, Miami's yuppies having a night on the town, and scores of Porsches and BMWs. It's one of the state's best neighborhoods for outdoor dining, seaside views, and people watching.

Take I-95 to US 41, then east to State A1A and turn north. Walking tours of the Deco District are offered each Saturday at 10:30 A.M. from 661 Washington Avenue. A fee is charged. Contact the Greater Miami Convention & Visitors Bureau, 701 Brickell Avenue, Miami, FL 33131. 800-283-2707.

Pass-a-Grille is the end of the road on the southern tip of St. Petersburg Beach, a quiet fishing village where clocks stopped ticking when the more glamorous, high-rise hotels were built up the beach. A hotel was built here in 1901, long before the still-glamorous Don CeSar was begun in the 1920s, but it was blown down in the 1921 hurricane. By 1911, a small fishing settlement had taken root.

Take a swim on one of the Gulf's great beaches, browse the shops, and have a fresh seafood meal. The sea views, which spread almost 360 degrees, are dazzling.

Take the Pinellas Bayway toll road off I-275 and turn left where Gulf Boulevard turns right.

Seaside, a new community between Destin and Panama City, is of interest because it is a totally planned, urban utopia of mock Victorian homes, red brick streets, and a scrubbed, prim demeanor. Unlike most other such developments in the state, this is more than a cluster of beachfront condos. It's a real community with

The planned community of Seaside

shops, a town hall, a post office, restaurants, an amphitheater, single-family homes, a couple of inns, and workshops.

Nightly rental rates are high, but weekly rates are a bargain, especially when several families share a five- or six-bedroom cottage.

Seaside has an upscale style all its own. The community even brought in an Ohio furniture designer to create the Seaside Look in furnishings and accessories. It's contrived, but the clean newness of it all is offbeat and appealing. Throughout the season, April through October, programs presented by the Seaside Institute include herb cooking lessons, jazz combos, artsy movies, and sea oats planting.

Seaside is located in the Panhandle on County 30A off US 98 between Grayton State Park and Seagrove Beach. 904-231-4224.

A settlement grew up where the **Steinhatchee** (pronounced "Steen-hatchee") River meets Deadman's Bay in the Gulf, and for a long time that was about the end of it. Today, however, the little end-of-the-world fishing village bustles with boats and new building projects. Stop by to snap a few photographs, do some scalloping or crabbing, soak up the salty ambience, and have a great seafood meal.

South on State 51 off US 19/98 west of Gainesville. For further information, contact the Taylor County Coastal Association, Box 789, Steinhatchee, FL 32359; 904-498-3513.

Settled by Greek sponge divers at the turn of the century, **Tarpon Springs** could be anywhere on the Mediterranean. It's dominated by the docks and by its Neo-Byzantine Greek Orthodox Cathedral. Men argue politics in Greek over tiny cups of strong coffee. Working shrimp and sponge boats, gaily painted with Greek motifs, shuttle in and out of the docks along Dodecanese Boulevard.

Stroll the waterfront, dine on moussaka and baklava, tour the sponge exhibits, and take a sightseeing cruise aboard the *St. Nicholas* to observe the old art of sponge diving. The ship is docked next to Spongeorama, a past-its-prime exhibit that nevertheless is part of the charm of this old Florida attraction. The Konger Coral Sea Aquarium at 852 Dodecanese Boulevard, in a 100,000-gallon tank, offers a look at the colorful life of sea creatures from the warm waters of the Gulf of Mexico.

Sponge divers at Tarpon Springs

Save time for the Greek-style tourist stalls, and stop at one of the hole-in-the-wall restaurants for take-out Greek food to eat on the beach at Fred Howard Park.

St. Nicholas Greek Orthodox Cathedral, built in 1943, is open daily. Please wear conservative attire if you come to see the fine marbles, artwork, and stained-glass windows. While you're dressed for church, also visit the Universalist Church, which has eleven paintings by American landscape painter George Inness Jr. It's open daily except on Mondays.

Tarpon Springs is northwest of Tampa on Alternate US 19. Come by road or take a day trip aboard the Clearwater Ferry out of Clearwater. For information, call the Tarpon Springs Chamber of Commerce at 813-937-6109. The Clearwater Ferry's number is 813-442-7433. The *St. Nicholas* sails daily at 10:30 A.M. and 4:30 P.M.; 813-937-9887. Casablanca Cruises offers dinner, dancing, and entertainment cruises on the Anclote River; 813-942-4452.

Yankeetown was probably settled by Union soldiers after the Civil War, and not much has happened since. A sun-scorched settlement at the end of a road to nowhere off US 19 along the lonely, shallow Gulf of Mexico north of Crystal River, it's within one of the state's most wildlife-rich areas. As you drive through, stop often to sweep the horizon with binoculars for views of birds or, perhaps, deer, and, with luck, a black bear.

The town is well off the highway, so it's not clogged with streams of cars. And the Gulf on this coast is so shallow that most transient boats stay well offshore, unlike the east coast, where every marina bristles with yachts from all over the world. What Yankeetown does have is good fishing and an impressive, ten-room fishing lodge with a dressy gourmet restaurant and a more casual seafood dining room. The Isaak Walton Lodge, built in 1927, will take you back to uncomplicated yesterdays when bedsteads were made out of iron, Florida hotels were paneled in termite-proof heart cypress, and hospitality was an art. Take County 40 west off US 19/98; 904-543-5567.

LOOK UP A DOWNTOWN

Many of Florida's oldest waterfront communities have in recent years grown away from the water, luring shoppers to distant malls and leaving historic schools, shops, and churches to wither. Some of these original waterfronts are still struggling to survive. Others have been restored and are once again in vogue. We've listed just a few.

Laidback and lazy, rustic and ramshackle, **Boca Grande** has been a fishing village since before the first white settlers arrived. Little has changed since then, unless you count the movie stars who come here to slum it in delicious anonymity. It's Margaritaville West, where a handful of natives love watching the passing parade of visitors.

Bicycles remain the favored mode of transport on the seven-mile road down the length of the island. Trendy boutiques have cute names like Special Effects, and restaurants tend to the gourmet with a touch of whimsy—grits served with Eggs Benedict, for example, and homemade ice cream at the Loose Caboose. The lighthouse dates to 1890. Gasparilla Island State Recreation Area is the place for beaching and picnicking. Take State 775 south from Venice to where it ends at the sea. For information, call the Boca Grande Chamber of Commerce. 813-964-0568.

In a four-block area of **Cocoa Village** you'll see a gothic church built in 1866, the 1916 Porcher House, a 1924 theater, and many other historic homes and shops. Take the docent-guided walking tour; 407-459-2200.

The speedway and malls have drawn visitors west while the beaches lure vacationers to the east, leaving the old downtown of **Daytona Beach** along the Halifax River a sweet reminder of the old days. The Kress Building is a Deco treasure; a regal old bank building has become a museum. With the development of the city marina into a waterfront festival marketplace, old Daytona is once again a picturesque gathering spot; 800-544-0415 or 904-255-0415. A good way to see the old downtown is aboard the Tiny Cruise Line; 904-226-2343.

DeLand, which long ago was founded along the St. Johns River, is now well inland. Drive into the heart of town, where turn-of-the-century buildings, many of them galleries and antique shops, line Woodland Boulevard. Just north of downtown are the stately old buildings of Stetson University. Its DeLand Hall is the oldest school building in continuous service in the state. Take any DeLand exit off I-4 or drive west out of

Daytona Beach on US 92, then south on US 17; 904-734-4331.

Restored in the old downtown section of **Delray Beach** is a school and theater complex called Old School Square. Its centerpiece is a 1913 schoolhouse, a remnant of early Florida seaside villages where slate blackboards were too expensive for pioneer farmers. They settled instead for walls painted black. Take the Delray Beach exit off I-95 between Boca Raton and Boynton Beach. 407-278-0424.

Islands in the Sun

All of them are named Island, but now that cars stream into Marco, Sanibel, Anastasia, Hutchinson, Amelia, and most of the Keys, it is important to know which islands you can reach only by boat and which ones you can reach by highway.

Keep in mind, too, when the word "island" sings a siren song to your city-weary soul, that lack of car access doesn't necessarily mean you'll have an island to yourself. Almost everyone in Florida has a boat, and on Sunday afternoons even some of the most remote islands can be crowded.

ISLANDS REACHED ONLY BY BOAT

Cabbage Key, located in Pine Island Sound off Fort Myers, was developed by mystery novelist Mary Roberts Rinehart in the 1930s. A ramshackle restaurant and bar is a good place to sit under a ceiling fan, dine on fresh fish, and think about running away to an island to write your own great novel. Tangled nature trails spread a visual feast of salt-tolerant vines and wildflowers. Many of the facilities are wheelchair accessible. Call 813-283-2278 for reservations and ferry information. Cruises that include Cabbage

Key are available from Captiva Cruises; 813-472-7549.

Caladesi Island State Park is one of the few big barrier islands on the Gulf coast that has not been developed. From downtown Clearwater or from docks on Honeymoon Island (which you can reach by road), take a ferry to the island and spend the day fishing, swimming the wave-washed Gulf beach, picnicking, and hiking nature trails through sandy scrubland filled with nature's clamor. There are rest rooms on the island; bring everything else with you. The park, 813-469-5918; Clearwater Ferry Service, 813-462-2628.

Special note: state park entry fees, charged by the carload, apply at Honeymoon Island; modest Caladesi Island entry fees are charged per person. The ferry tour to Caladesi allows you four hours on the island; if you want a full-day beach experience, arrive early and spend part of the day on Honeymoon Island, then complete your day there after the ferry returns.

Cayo Costa State Park, just south of Boca Grande, can be reached only by ferry. Beachcomb along miles of beach, hike through stands of pine and palm, and train your binoculars on subtropical birds by the dozen. Shelling during the winter months is outstanding. Come at low tide, preferably after a scrappy west wind. The island offers primitive camping, picnic areas, and rental cabins. For ferry information, call 813-964-0375.

Cumberland Island National Seashore is actually in Georgia, but it's within swimming distance of Fernandina Beach, and that's where you'll be picked up if you want to stay at the Greyfield Inn. You can also reach the island from St. Marys, Georgia, by park service ferry, for a fee.

One of the most aloof and natural islands of the chain known as Georgia's Golden Isles, Cumberland has a history that goes back to Indian times. A Spanish mission operated here for eighty years during the 1500s.

The island is so remote and natural today, it's hard to believe that it has such a long, rich history. Nathanael Greene, a Revolutionary War general, began building a home here in 1786. Gen. "Light-Horse Harry" Lee also lived and died here. Taken ill at sea, he made port at Cumberland, where he was cared for by Louisa Shaw, mistress of Dungeness. The Thomas Carnegie family built a lavish mansion on the island before the Civil War. In 1898, the thirty-room Greek Revival

Cabbage Key is a great place to write your own novel

mansion Plum Orchard was Lucy Carnegie's wedding gift to her son.

The barrier island has sixteen miles of beaches, mountainous dunes, and tangled forests of wind-sculpted live oaks. Walking its endless paths, you'll see wildlife of all kinds, including wild horses. On a ranger-guided tour you'll see the ruins of the Carnegie mansion and other historic sites in addition to the wildlife. Swim the beach and stay on in the primitive campground if you like. Everything you need must be brought with you. Reservations to ride the ferry are essential.

For ferry reservations: 912-882-4335. For reservations at the nine-room Greyfield Inn, which offers American Plan dining to its guests: 912-882-4335. Guests can be picked up by boat from St. Marys or from Fernandina Beach.

Deerfield Park Island in the Intracoastal Waterway in heavily populated south Florida is an unpeopled pocket far from the madding crowd. Today it's simply a good nature hike, but its story is intriguing. During Prohibition, when Al Capone and his crooked cronies frequented the casino at the Riverview Restaurant, he decided to buy the island. Before a deal could be struck, Capone was collared, and the little island remains today a refuge for shorebirds and raccoons. Free ferries come to the island twice a week in season from the Riverview, 1741 Riverview Road, Deerfield Beach. 305-428-3463. The restaurant closes in summer.

While you're in the neighborhood, schedule a dinner at Cap's Place, which can be reached by ferry from Lighthouse Point. It's operated by Cap Knight, a former rumrunner. In its heyday, when it was an illegal gambling joint, its guests included Winston Churchill and Franklin D. Roosevelt. The ambience is South Seas; the seafood is superb. 305-941-0418.

Dog Island is one of the barrier islands in the Gulf of Mexico off Apalachicola, a lonely community that enjoys some of the best beaching and birding in the world. Get a boat (out of the marina on US 98 in Carrabelle) to bring you over and spend a day on the beaches and nature paths. Bring everything you'll need with you.

A few cottages nestle among the sand dunes, which are among the tallest in the state, but if you want to stay overnight there's only one bed and breakfast. Reservations are essential and can be hard to arrange because the proprietor has only a cellular phone that's sometimes out of order. It all adds to the sense of privileged getaway, so persevere in arranging a stay here. 800-451-5294.

Egmont Key State Park, a 440-acre wildlife refuge, has the only lighthouse in the United States that still has a human lighthouse tender. The island served as a prisoner-of-war camp during the third Seminole war and was captured by the Union during the Civil War. Today it's a lonely outpost guarding the entrance to Tampa Bay. For ferry information: 813-893-2627.

Elliott Key is one of a long string of barrier islands in Biscayne Bay National Park. Most of the park lies underwater. This long, slender island is reached by a tour boat that runs on Sundays from December to May. The solitude on the island isn't quite what you expect because it's very popular with people who come in their own boats. And everyone in Florida has a boat.

Nonetheless, it's a breezy and beautiful boat ride to an island that has great beaches and six miles of good hiking trails through sands and scrub.

Excursion boats leave from Convoy Point, which is east of Homestead on North Canal Drive. 305-247-2400.

Fort Jefferson National Monument crowns one of Florida's most haunting islands. The Florida Keys don't really stop at Key West, where the road ends. They straggle on into the Gulf of Mexico for miles more, first in a group known as the Marquesas and then the Dry Tortugas. Pirates loved hiding out among the scattered, featureless cays so much that by 1846, the United States chose this strategic spot to build a fort to guard the entrance to the Gulf of Mexico from pirates and other invaders.

As a fortress, Fort Jefferson was an enormous flop. Cisterns, the only source of fresh water, leaked. The brick walls of the fort were obsolete before they were finished because new, rifled cannons could shoot through them.

As a historic site, however, the fort has a major claim to fame. Turned into a military prison, Fort Jefferson housed Dr. Samuel Mudd, who was convicted (probably wrongly) as a conspirator in the Lincoln assassination. Yellow fever ravaged the prison time and again, and for his heroism in treating fever victims, Mudd was eventually set free.

Now the cool, shadowy dungeons of the fort are a tourist attraction. The key is also one of the best bird-watching sites in Florida because migrating birds stop here to rest on their long flights between North and South America. It's one of the largest sooty tern nesting spots in the world.

Camping is permitted, but you must bring all your own supplies, including water. Access is only by boat or seaplane. To reach the park superintendent: 305-242-7700; for transportation information: 800-FLA-KEYS.

Fort Matanzas National Monument sprawls over 298 acres of Anastasia and Rattlesnake Islands, a seascape of black waters and waving reeds that turn toast colored in the pitiless sun. It was near here that early French Huguenot settlers were massacred by the Spanish, and the name Matanzas, or slaughter, remained. The Spanish fortified the site, which guards the entry to St. Augustine, and it was also occupied by the English. When Florida became part of the United States in 1821, however, the fort was abandoned and forgotten until restoration began in 1916.

Today it's an island of tranquillity in contrast to the bold seductions of St. Augustine's old city. Arrive on the free ferry, tour the visitors center, and listen for ghosts in the cool, dark, echoing turrets and tunnels.

Take the ferry from Anastasia Island, fourteen miles south of St. Augustine. 904-471-0116 or 829-6506. The site is open daily except Christmas.

Hontoon Island State Park admission costs no more than standard Florida state park entry fees, but the deal includes a short ferry ride across the St. Johns River. Timucuan Indians built a 300-foot-long ceremonial mound on this sacred island centuries ago. Divers continue to dig up Indian artifacts from the primeval ooze of the riverbed. A replica of one of the totems, an extremely rare find, is on display at the island.

Bring a picnic lunch to eat under a huge live oak tree, and tent camp overnight if you like. The park has a marina that is popular with private boaters, along with hiking trails, rest rooms, and an observation tower that has a bird's-eye view of the St. Johns River.

Six miles southwest of DeLand off State 44. 904-736-5309.

Indian Key State Historic Site. When you set foot on lonely Indian Key, it's hard to picture it pulsing with life, warehouses, cattle, homes, and families. The story really begins centuries ago, when unknown Indians lived here on the fruits of the sea. Modern history began in 1770 when, it is said, 400 French settlers were massacred here by the Calusa Indians.

By the late eighteenth century, salvagers, working the many ships that wrecked on the reefs off the Keys, were thriving in Key West. It's said that per capita income there was higher than anywhere else in the United States. Wrecker Jacob Housman had had a falling out with other salvagers in Key West, so he set up his own operation here on Indian Key. So prosperous were his wharves and warehouses that his island became for a time the county seat of Dade County. Dr. Henry Perrine, a physician with an interest in tropical botany, moved to the island to experiment with agave, tea, mangoes, and other plantings.

It all ended in one horrible holocaust in 1840, when Seminole Indians on the rampage torched the island and murdered many of its inhabitants, including Dr. Perrine. The exact death toll will never be known because slaves at the time were considered chattel; no one knows if they were counted among the human dead.

Three-hour boat tours come to Indian Key Thursday through Monday at 8:30 A.M. All that remains of Housman's empire are some ruins, but the plants brought here by Dr. Perrine continue to cover the island. Call for reservations. 305-664-4815.

Lignumvitae Key State Botanical Site, reached by boat tours from Indian Key, is a 280-acre treasury of hardwood forests of the type usually found in the Caribbean, not Florida. The three-hour round-trip boat tour includes a one-hour guided walk around the island. Tours are offered from Thursday through Monday. 305-664-4815.

North and South Grange Islands. Found in the Indian River, these two islands in the heart of the Merritt Island National Wildlife Refuge are unequaled spots for watching bird life, including the endangered brown pelican. Both islands have rustic campsites, rest rooms, and picnic facilities; the north island also has a boat dock. Landing is not permitted on Pelican Island, but it has been a wildlife sanctuary since 1903, and bird-watching is superb. For information about getting to the islands, call the Cocoa Beach Tourism Council at 407-459-2200.

Little Palm Island in the Florida Keys is a fantasy island where movie stars go to unwind and gourmets go to dine on smoked salmon parfait, grilled tuna, lobster and stone crab soup, and chocolate ravioli stuffed with coconut cream. The flavor is South Seas; the price range for suites in this lost-world hideaway is Ultra Expensive. Hosts pick up guests at Little Torch Key, MM 28.5.; 305-872-2524 or 800-3-GET LOST.

St. Vincent National Wildlife Refuge covers an island in the Gulf of Mexico. Although local marinas offer boat service for the short hop to the island, it's best to sign up for ranger-guided tours that are offered for only a few days a year, usually in October. Aboard a barge that can hold up to twenty-eight people, you'll be taken to the island and then taken on a tour by farm wagon that covers the entire, nine-mile length of the island. The whole tour lasts about five hours, and you must bring lunch, water, and (if possible) a life preserver.

Obviously, the island isn't overrun by tourism, which gives its few visitors an inside track to see nature in the raw. Bald eagles soar overhead, wild turkeys roam the scrub, and loggerhead turtles come ashore to nest.

Take County 30, off US 98 between Apalachicola and Port St. Joe, and follow the signs to the refuge access at Indian Pass Peninsula. Call 904-653-8808 for information about the next nature cruise.

ISLANDS TO REACH BY ROADS

Amelia Island (see Fernandina Beach in Chapter 6.)

Discovery Island is a real find. Only the Disney people could pull off an attraction that is this natural, credible, and good in the heart of a major theme park. Boats take passengers to the island from the Magic Kingdom or Fort Wilderness to stroll among tropical forests filled with colorful birds, dazzling plantings, and nature exhibits. This is a separate theme park, with its own admission. With a ticket, you can stay all day if you like. 407-824-3783.

You can reach **Honeymoon Island State Recreation Area** by road, but it's also served by ferries, which are more fun. Once called Hog Island, it was renamed by developers in the 1930s who built thatched huts on the island to rent to romantics. On the island are one of the state's last remaining stands of virgin slash pine, an abundance of bird and marine life, and a superb beach on the Gulf of Mexico. It's located at the end of State 586 north of Dunedin. 813-469-5942.

Jupiter Island is the home of some ultra-exclusive estates and security is tight, so don't wander off State A1A to go sightseeing. The two reasons to come here are to see Blowing Rocks Preserve, a bouldery beachfront where spume shoots up between the rocks, and Hobe Sound Beach, which is part of the Hobe Sound National Wildlife Refuge. Both are best at low tide, when shelling is best at Hobe Sound and more rocks are exposed at Blowing Rock.

Take County 707 east from Hobe Sound, which is south of Stuart, and turn north at the ocean to Hobe Sound Beach, then backtrack south on 707 to Blowing Rock. Hobe Sound Chamber of Commerce: 407-546-4724; Hobe Sound National Wildlife Refuge, administered by Loxahatchee: 407-546-6141.

Salty and sophisticated, **Key West** is a world apart, different from anything else in Florida or even in the Keys. Discovered by the Spanish, who probably named it Cayo Hueso ("cay of bones"),

it's the end of the long, long Overseas Highway that strings the necklace of keys together. Sunset, always spelled with a capital S, is celebrated each evening at Mallory Docks. It's wacky and free, and not to be missed.

For centuries, Key West developed independently from the United States. An island, it had closer relations with the Bahamas, which were a well-developed British maritime colony, than with the mainland of Florida, which was a buggy backwater with no sizable settlements south of St. Augustine.

Ships ran aground so frequently along the coast that Key West's professional wreckers grew enormously wealthy. Some called it luck; others whispered that false lights were set out sometimes to lure ships onto the rocks.

During the boom, great mansions were built, many of them prefabricated in the Bahamas and shipped here to be assembled. In one, the entire third floor is a ballroom. Others were lavishly appointed with spiral staircases, leaded glass, and glowing mahogany furniture, much of it salvaged from unfortunate ships.

Everything changed when railroad pioneer Henry Flagler brought his tracks across the sea all the way to Key West. A grand hotel, the Casa Marina, was built to house wealthy tourists. People and goods poured in. All that ended in the 1930s when the railroad and most of its bridges were swept away in a hurricane. America's richest city became, in one census, the poorest.

The railbed was replaced by a road, but Key West maintains its cocky, aloof, island flavor. To be unconventional here is not just tolerated, it's almost a house rule. Although it sounds touristy, the best way to start a visit here is aboard either the Conch Train or the Old Town Trolley. Key West is a walking city. After taking the tour you'll have a better idea of where you want to go on foot. It's well worth the time and shoe leather to stroll up one street and down the next for as long as your feet hold up.

Stop to see Ernest Hemingway's home, where descendants of his six-toed cats still live. Tour the 1847 lighthouse and lighthouse keeper's home, which have been meticulously restored. See the Little White House, where great political dramas were played out during the Truman administration. Shop the many markets, especially Key West Hand Print Fabrics, the perfume factory,

and Kino sandals. Inexpensive and practical, the sandals are a Key West tradition.

See the home where Audubon lived and painted a century ago. Visit Mel Fisher's Maritime Heritage Society Museum to see a dazzling display of treasures Fisher has brought up from the sea. The Key West Aquarium, built in the 1930s, features tropical fish from local waters. The historic Turtle Kraals, once the butchering spot for turtles, is now a rehabilitation center for turtles and seabirds. Key West is filled with hotels, inns, restaurants, and bars in all price ranges.

Drive south from Miami until the road ends. The Overseas Highway is also US 1. For more information, call 800-FLA-KEYS.

Only a few decades ago, **Marco Island** couldn't be reached by road. Overrun with snakes and swarming with mosquitoes, it was braved by only the most stalwart nature lovers. Today, however, there's a causeway to the island, and ease of access has brought construction crews that have covered the island with smart neighborhoods.

Today, the snakes are gone and the mosquitoes are under control. The beach is lined with fine hotels, and the island bristles with fine

*Hemingway's house
in Key West*

restaurants, shops, and galleries. To capture the flavor of Old Marco, take a self-guided driving tour that stops at marked locales. One marker indicates the site of a school that was built here in 1889.

Calusa Indians fished these islands and had an abundant life here. Some of their shell mounds form hills high enough to have sheltered them from high waters during hurricanes. At fifty-one feet above sea level, Indian Hill is the highest elevation in southwestern Florida. At the turn of the century, it was the site of the Heights Hotel.

An outstanding restaurant, the Olde Marco Inn, has been on its site since 1883. The old inn is a National Historic Site. It's at 100 Palm Street and is open daily. Reservations are recommended. 813-394-3131.

Take Goodland Road to find an end-of-the-world fishing village. Said to be one of the earliest-named places in North America, Good Land appears on maps made by the earliest Spanish explorers. For information, call the Marco Island Chamber of Commerce at 813-394-7549.

Sanibel and **Captiva** are often lumped together by travel writers because the toll causeway leads to Sanibel, which must be driven for its entire length before a bridge takes you onto Captiva and the end of the road. The farther you drive out into this seagirt Eden, the more the sense of heady getaway. One of Florida's largest and most complete resorts is South Seas Island Plantation on Captiva. It is one-stop vacation shopping for golf, tennis, sailing lessons, restaurants, a variety of accommodations, cruises, and even a resortwide transportation system.

Closer to the mainland, and perfect for a pampered beachfront vacation in serene, European-style surroundings, is Song of the Sea on Sanibel, where innkeeper Patricia Slater serves fresh fruit and French pastries each morning. Take your breakfast poolside, to the garden or beach, or carry it back in your suite.

Sanibel and Captiva are best known for seashell finds, but they also have a long list of sightseeing stops, including a museum and the "Ding" Darling Wildlife Refuge. Choose from shops, restaurants, and beaches galore.

For information contact the Lee Island Coast Visitor and Convention Bureau, 2180 West First Street, Fort Myers, FL 33902. 813-338-3500 or 800-237-6444.

Big and Little Talbot Island State Parks

are found in the northeasternmost notch of the state north of Jacksonville. The reed-rimmed island is geographically part of the chain known as Georgia's Golden Isles. Mazes of waterways, some of them deep and swift running and others shallow and sluggish, weave through miles of marsh grasses that gleam golden in low sun.

Along its Atlantic side, Little Talbot has five miles of scrubbed beach firm enough for good jogging but also soft and smooth enough for snoozing in the sun. Along the marsh side, tidal streams abound with mullet, striped bass, redfish, and sheepshead. The island has campsites, picnic areas, and hiking paths. It's on State A1A. Cross the St. Johns on the Mayport ferry and go north on A1A or cross by bridge at Jacksonville and go east on State 105. 904-251-2320.

Included in the complex is Fort George State Cultural Site, which shows traces of continuous human occupation for at least 5,000 years. On this island, sixty-five-foot Mount Cornelia is the highest point on the Atlantic coast south of Sandy Hook, New Jersey. Big Talbot Island State Park is immediately north of Little Talbot Island State Park.

One of the Gulf's finest barrier islands, the long sandspit that is St. George Island has a nine-mile beach that looks like it was freshly laid down by a salt shaker. Swim the warm, emerald waters. Look for snowy plovers and willets. Hike the boardwalks to look for wildlife in the grassy flats, and look for seashells. They are so abundant and varied you can come away with an impressive collection. **St. George Island State Park** is ten miles southeast of Eastpoint, off US 98. 904-927-2111.

Festivals by the Sea

Unless stated otherwise, admission at the following events is free.

NIGHTLY

Most Floridians, especially those along the Gulf coast, gather on waterfront patios and in tiki bars to watch the sun set, but Sunset in **Key West** is something else again. Tourists and locals alike gather at **Mallory Docks** to watch the sun go down. As it slips into the sea, they applaud its performance.

While you wait for the last loom of the sun to disappear below the horizon, you can shop the peddlers, have a massage, tip a juggler, sip from your hip flask, listen to street musicians, dance with a stranger, and otherwise take part in the wacky, uninhibited fun. Check the almanac for the time, then show up about half an hour before sundown.

JANUARY

Blue Spring State Park in **Orange City**, one of the best places to spot manatee in winter, hosts its annual **Manatee Festival** the last weekend of the month. On view all year is the original homestead, now restored. During the festival, lumberjacks compete, wildlife handlers bring their exhibits, Indians dance, and environmentalists set up education displays. 904-775-1112.

Epiphany, an important holy day in the Greek Orthodox Church, is celebrated at the docks in **Tarpon Springs** in traditional Greek style, including the dive for the golden cross. 813-937-6109.

Sandestin in the Panhandle stirs up the **Great Southern Gumbo Cook-Off**. Restaurants from throughout northwest Florida compete. Attendees cast ballots for the three best seafood gumbos in the contest. 800-822-6877.

Free **water-ski shows** can be seen off **Bayfront Marina** in **Sarasota** on Sundays January through March. 813-957-1877 or 800-522-9799.

FEBRUARY

Tampa Bay is invaded year after year in one of the zaniest, oldest maritime fiestas in the states, the **Gasparilla Festival**, which has been a tradition since the turn of the century. In memory of pirate Jose Gaspar, a huge fleet of pirate boats descends on the city while merrymakers ashore and afloat party madly. It's a month-long series of races, tournaments, and fun, highlighted by the invasion and parade. 800-44-TAMPA.

The **Miami Boat Show**, held in **Miami Beach** mid-month, is the largest boat show in the United States and the second largest in the world. In various venues around the island, you'll see hundreds of boats indoors and out, oceans of equipment and accessories, squads of experts, dozens of booths, and thousands of attendees from all over the world. Florida has many good boat shows, but this one is also an important international nautical event. 305-531-8410.

MARCH

Ferdinand DeSoto "discovers" the Manatee River year after year in a week-long celebration in **Bradenton** that reenacts his landing here in 1539. 813-747-1998.

Fort Myers Beach celebrates its **Shrimp Festival** for an entire week in early March. The

Wait for the shrimp boats to come in,
laden down with their catch

festivities end with the Blessing of the Fleet. 813-463-6451.

The **Greek Food and Wine Festival** in **Tarpon Springs** is sponsored by the American Hellenic Educational Progressive Society with traditional food, song, dance, and arts along the riverfront. 813-937-6109.

The **Port Canaveral Seafood Festival and Great Chowder Cook-off** is one of the largest and most luscious seafood feasts on the Florida's east coast. This annual festival features smoked and fresh fish, gumbo, chowder, rock shrimp, blue crab, and a cooking contest to choose the county's biggest chowderhead. Cocoa Beach Tourism Council, 407-459-2200.

Naples is the only place in Florida where you can see **swamp buggy races**. These awkward vehicles spend the rest of their useful lives carrying tourists to the most remote corners of the state's marshes. Noisy and hilarious, the event is telecast worldwide. 813-774-2701.

Sanibel, home of some of the best shelling in Florida, has been hosting an annual **Shell Fair** since the 930s. Awards are given for displays and collections, and schoolchildren make up a special display of live shells. 813-472-2155.

APRIL

On the first weekend after Easter, **A Taste of Jacksonville** gathers at the Riverwalk along the St. Johns River to eat international food specialties, dance, listen to music, see a boat show, and view the Blessing of the Fleet as boats and yachts stream past by the dozen. 904-396-4900.

Mid-month marks the **Fort Walton Beach Seafood Festival**, focusing on the Gulf's freshest and most delicious catches. Music, arts and crafts, and other down-home events complete the three-day blowout. Admission is charged. 800-322-3319 or 904-651-7131.

Hialeah gathers around the Miami River for its annual **River Cities Festival** during the third weekend of the month. Miccosukee Indians turn out with their dances and crafts, and there's plenty of food, entertainment, and boat racing. 305-539-3000.

Panama City looks out over the Gulf of Mexico as sixty brutish powerboats compete in the annual **Gulf Coast Offshore Powerboat Races** in late April/early May. This event, a fundraiser, attracts 75 to 80 hydroplanes, 60 powerboats, and 100,000 people. 904-785-0561.

Pompano Beach and **Fort Lauderdale**, both in Broward County, have superb **seafood festivals** this month. Restaurants bring their best seafood recipes. Browse the booths while listening to live music, looking over crafts booths, entering contests, and copping a tan. Fort Lauderdale, 305-463-4431; Pompano Beach, 305-941-2940.

Marathon takes its name seriously as it hosts a **foot race** in which runners from all over the world cross the famous Seven Mile Bridge. 305-743-8513.

EASTER

Cocoa Beach, the surfing capital of Florida, takes to the beach on Easter weekend to hang ten. Groove to live music and watch the **surfers compete** for titles and prizes. Cocoa Beach Tourism Council, 407-459-2200.

Daytona's Easter Beach Run on the Saturday before Easter attracts 2,000 runners in 26 divisions. The hard-packed sands, where motorcars once set speed records, are the ideal surface for running. Easter Day begins with a sunrise service at the historic, oceanfront band shell. 904-258-3106.

Ormond Beach's **Art Show on the Halifax River** spreads along the lawns of the Casements, once the winter home of John D. Rockefeller. More than 200 artists exhibit. While you're art browsing, stop at the International Food Court for body fuel. 904-677-6362.

MAY

Daytona Beach is the perfect place for an **International Kite Festival**. Champion flyers from all over the world come to the "world's most famous beach" to compete for speed, stunts, aerobatics, and other skills. Children have their own kite-flying area. Arts, crafts, and food complete the festive scene. 904-255-0415 or 800-544-0415.

The **Mayfest** in **Destin** has a Cajun flavor as trumpets, clarinets, and saxes send their sounds out over the bayous. Spicy Creole specialties are the culinary order of the day. 904-651-7131 or 800-322-3319.

A **Seafood Festival** as only **Tarpon Springs** can spring it is a good excuse for coming in May to this quaint Mediterranean village where the Anclote River meets the Gulf. 813-937-6109.

The **Isle of Eight Flags Shrimp Festival** in early May includes a Blessing of the Fleet, a mock pirate attack, an arts and crafts fair, and shrimp fresh from the fleet that headquarters here in downtown **Fernandina Beach**. 904-277-0727.

Fort Walton Beach is the home of the annual **Hog's Breath Hobie Regatta**. The event, which attracts 200 brightly colored catamaran sailboats and thousands of spectators, begins the night before with an all-night pig roast. 800-322-3319 or 904-651-7131.

Jacksonville turns back the clock to the **old riverboat days** with period costumes, replicas of historic ships, music, and entertainers. The event also brings artists and crafters to the Riverwalk. 904-630-3900.

Palatka on the St. Johns River is the home of a 38.5-mile sailboat race to Jacksonville. The **Mug Race**, made more fun by the fluky winds and currents of the river, is silly and fun rather than serious yachting. Usually held the first Friday of May, the event features live bands, food, and prizes. 904-264-4094.

MEMORIAL DAY WEEKEND

The **Sun-Dek Surfing Contest** brings 35,000 spectators and surfing's hottest competitors to Indialantic. Cocoa Beach Tourism Council, 407-459-2200.

JUNE

The **Billy Bowlegs Festival**, named for a Seminole Indian chief, brings 500 pirate boats to invade **Fort Walton Beach**. The festival features games, pageants, the crowning of the queen, treasure hunts, and more. 800-322-3319.

The Miami-Budweiser Unlimited **Hydroplane Regatta** in **Miami**'s Marine Stadium pits the world's fastest and most brutish big speedboats against each other in a run for the Governor's Trophies. 305-361-6730.

The **Annual International Submarine Races** are a sort of maritime version of solar-power car races. Teams from all over the world race human-powered submarines off **Fort Lauderdale**. 305-351-4175.

Madeira Beach's swimming-running-bicycling **Triathlon** is an athletic spectacle. 813-391-7373.

Sandcastle building is a state passion, but it takes on mammoth proportions and big prizes each June in **St. Petersburg Beach**. 813-360-1881.

Southern Ocean Racing, a showcase of sailboats, takes place off **St. Petersburg**. 813-821-6164.

4TH OF JULY

You can view fireworks displays, usually preceded by fun and games, from virtually every major waterfront in the state. The waterfront displays are most spectacular because you get a double dose as the sparklers reflect in the water.

Oceanfront Park in **Daytona Beach** is as beachy a site as can be found for **feasting, music and fireworks**. The old-fashioned Band Shell here dates to the 1920s. Bring a picnic, pick up snacks on the Boardwalk, or try one of the elegant beachside restaurants. 904-253-0254.

Jazzmatazz in **Ormond Beach** showcases some of the area's best jazz musicians as well as a few national headliners. The celebration features fun for the children, plenty of food, and jazz until the fireworks start. Bring a chair or blanket to the Casements, overlooking the Halifax River. 904-677-6362.

JULY

The world's only underwater symphony plays for this annual **Underwater Music Festival** at the Looe Key National Marine Sanctuary in **Big Pine Key**. 305-872-2411. Bring your scuba gear.

Fort Lauderdale's **Sandblast** is a sand sculpture contest that brings in plenty of talent. Bring your camera and capture the glory before the tides wash it all away. 305-761-5388.

Sarasota celebrates for a week with parades, boat shows, and entertainments before its **Offshore Grand Prix** powerboat races. 813-955-9009.

AUGUST

On the weekend before Labor Day, **Sarasota**'s **Sailing Squadron Labor Day Regatta** is the largest one-design regatta held on Florida's Gulf Coast. 813-388-2355.

LABOR DAY WEEKEND

In this annual fundraiser, **surfers gather** at Florida's best surfing beach, **Cocoa Beach**, to show their stuff. Everyone's invited to see the action, listen to live music, and share the food and fun. Cocoa Beach Tourism Council, 407-459-2200.

Las Olas, **Fort Lauderdale**'s ritziest boulevard and home of its most important art shows, spreads its annual **Las Olas Labor Day Art Fair** up and down the street this weekend. 305-472-3755.

SEPTEMBER

Daytona Beach knows **beach volleyball**. This yearly event attracts top AVP-ranked players to Oceanfront Park, where they play for King of the Beach honors. 404-395-3500.

King Neptune's Seafood Harvest hits the riverfront at **Daytona Beach** during the last weekend in the month. Environmental displays, music, and crafts set the scene for oceans of succulent seafood. 904-258-8972.

The annual **St. Johns River Festival**, held on the river west of **DeLand**, is a wonderfully wacky race of rafts that teams put together out of beer cans, milk cartons, and anything else that will float. It's hometown hoopla with fun and food for the whole family, mid-month. 904-734-4371.

The **Pensacola Seafood Festival**, held at **Pensacola Beach**, is a carnival of food vendors, music, games, and crafts, all focusing on seafood fresh from local fishing fleets. 800-343-4321 (in Florida) or 800-874-1234 (outside Florida).

The **Sarasota/Bradenton Blues Festival** brings crowds to the riverfront park to listen to national and regional blues and gospel greats. 813-746-5989.

OCTOBER

The **First Coast Maritime Exhibition**, held in the Flag Pavilion at **Jacksonville Beach**, brings together items from local museums and on loan from other museums to create an important display of maritime art and artifacts. 904-798-9148.

*Enjoy sportfishing
any time of year*

Beach Fest takes to the sands of **St. Petersburg Beach** on the first weekend of the month. Ashore you'll find entertainment and food; offshore there's a powerboat race. 813-360-6957.

Seafest along **Jacksonville**'s Riverwalk is a seafood festival featuring the specialties of dozens of local restaurants. Music fills the air, and 50,000 people turn out for the fun. 904-798-9148.

Cedar Key's **Seafood Festival** combines the best in fresh Gulf fish, crab, and oysters with the picturebook quaintness of a village that time has passed by. It usually takes place on the third weekend. 904-543-5549.

Niceville in the Panhandle is the home of the **Boggy Bayou Mullet Festival**, where 11 tons of flopping-fresh mullet will be eaten while 300,000 diners enjoy pageants, contests, music, and such spectacles as rattlesnake milking and the crowning of the Mullet Queen. 800-322-3319.

The entire month is filled with **Destin**'s **Fishing Rodeo**, attracting 1,000 anglers aboard sleek, gleaming sportfishing boats.

Panama City Beach hosts its annual **Indian Summer Seafood Festival**, featuring 100 arts and crafts vendors, top-name entertainers, fireworks, parachute jumps, and seafood fresh

from the Gulf. It usually takes place on the second weekend. 904-234-0292.

Port Canaveral, one of Florida's major seaports and home port to some major cruise ships, celebrates its two-day **Port Weekend**. Events include races ashore and afloat, music, arts and crafts, and tours of visiting military vessels. Cocoa Beach Tourism Council, 407-459-2200.

NOVEMBER

Apalachicola, Florida's oystering capital, has its **Florida Seafood Festival** with parades, oyster eating, a shucking contest, music, and games on the first Saturday of the month. Especially colorful is the blessing of the fleet as it passes in review. 904-653-9419.

Yacht races sponsored by the **Clearwater Yacht Club** attract more than 100 yachts of all sizes to vie for the **Kahlua Cup**. 813-461-0011.

Fort Myers Beach has a **sand sculpting contest** that has been named one of the top twenty events in the Southeast. Individuals, teams, masters, and mudpie amateurs fill the beach with castles, creatures, and creations of all sizes and motifs while onlookers eat, drink, listen to nationally known entertainers, and make merry. 800-782-9283.

Gulf Beaches Arts and Crafts Festival is held in **Kolb Park, Indian Rocks Beach**. More than 175 artists and crafters exhibit their wares while you stroll in the sun and seabreeze. 813-595-4575.

DECEMBER

Fernandina Beach celebrates a **Victorian Seaside Christmas** all month with lights, tours of historic homes, Teddy Bear teas, and much more. 800-2-AMELIA.

Jensen Beach was settled by a Danish sailor who began to raise pineapple. It's not a local crop today, but the city celebrates its **Pineapple Festival** on the second weekend of the month with a street fair, a parade, and rides. 407-334-3444.

Key Largo goes Caribbean for three days during the second weekend of the month to celebrate **Island Jubilee** with arts and crafts, Caribbean and Creole cuisine, music, and folderol. 305-451-1414.

Sanford is the site of the **largest inland sailing regatta** in the nation as more than 700 entrants compete on six courses around Lake Monroe. The weekend festival includes sailing clinics, races, food, and entertainment. 407-425-0585.

Christmas boat parades are held in the following locations:

DeLand, 904-734-4331; **Destin**, 904-651-7131 or 800-322-3319; **Fort Lauderdale**, 305-527-8750; **Jacksonville**, 904-798-9148; **Madeira Beach**, (Boca Ciega Bay), 813-391-7373; and **Tampa** (Alafia River), 813-677-2604.

Music rings across the St. Johns River from **Jacksonville Landing** at noon every day during the Christmas season. Concerts are free. 904-798-9148.

SEASIDE FESTIVAL MARKETPLACES

Trendy shopping and dining complexes, often called festival marketplaces, have transformed some of America's scruffiest waterfronts into showplaces frequented by locals and tourists alike. In Florida, where the waterfront is never far away, leisurely seaside grazing has long been a way of life; the seaside festival goes on all year.

Below we list some of the best of Florida's waterfront marketplaces. Some are slick and sophisticated; others are small and salty. Whatever the atmosphere, you can have a coffee at an outdoor café, shop chic stores, catch a water taxi to your next appointment, sit on a park bench and gaze out to sea, listen to a free concert, and stay on for dinner at a stellar restaurant.

Bayside Marketplace covers sixteen acres in the heart of downtown **Miami** overlooking Biscayne Bay. Browse among 150 shops, take in a show at one of the two pavilions, nosh among the pushcarts or make reservations for a four-star dinner, and stroll a waterfront that bristles with masts and outriggers. The marketplace is part of Bayfront Park with its flowering trees and monuments, a laser tower, and an amphitheater where big-name performers often perform.

The departure point for many of the area's cruises and the home of a sportfishing fleet, Bayfront throbs with life from first light, when the fishermen take off for the deep seas, to the late dining hours. 305-577-3344.

Boatyard Village, **Clearwater**, is a recreated Victorian-era fishing village overlooking a cozy cove in Tampa Bay. Try the restaurants, shop the boutiques and galleries, enjoy the free entertainments that are frequently scheduled here, and take in a show at the playhouse. The complex is open from 10:00 A.M. to 5:00 P.M. daily at 16100 Fairchild Drive. 813-535-4678.

Head out to sea without leaving terra firma by strolling **Cocoa Beach Pier**, which stretches 800 feet out into the Atlantic. Although many communities have lengthy piers for fishing, this one also has shops and restaurants. It's a favorite location for festivals and other special events throughout the year. It's at 401 Meade Avenue. 407-783-7549.

Garrison Seaport Center (grand opening: 1995) is **Tampa**'s 20.5-acre complex with shops, a cruise ship terminal, a cinema complex, restaurants, and a music arena as well as the landmark Florida Aquarium.

Hamlin's Landing in **Indian Rocks Beach** is a Victorian-style complex along the Gulf-side Intracoastal Waterway. Have lunch, shop, then take a dining and dancing evening cruise aboard the *Starlite Princess*, a 106-foot paddle wheeler.

Jacksonville Landing overlooks the St. Johns River, where you can arrive by water taxi, car, or automated Skyway Express. The two-story mall has sixty nationally known chain stores that sell jewelry, clothing, gifts, luggage, accessories, and gourmet cooking equipment. The 10,000-square-foot TILT's Ostrich Landing amusement center offers a family boardwalk, a shooting gallery, and video games. The Landing, across the street from the Omni Hotel, is the home of Juliette's, a garden restaurant famed for its Sunday brunches. 904-353-9736.

Jacksonville Riverwalk, just across the river from Jacksonville Landing, is a long drive away from the north bank of the river but only a quick hop by water taxi to find more hotels, restaurants, and shops. Stroll the wide, mile-long walkway on the river, open a picnic lunch, aim your camera across the water to capture the downtown skyline, and visit the Navy Memorial. Friendship Fountain, at the end of the Riverwalk, is said to be the largest fountain in the world. It's a splashy display by day and a carnival of lights by night. 904-353-9736.

John's Pass Village and Boardwalk at **Madeira Beach** is a rustic shopping and dining center in the midst of a bustling waterfront and fishing fleet home port. Commercial and pleasure boats come and go while you browse the galleries or enjoy a frosty drink. You'll find it at 12921 Gulf Boulevard East. 813-397-7242.

The Pier is a **St. Petersburg** landmark that looks like a five-story pyramid turned upside-down. Rooftop dining looks out over Tampa Bay; indoors, you'll find one of the famous Columbia restaurants serving some of the best paella in the state. Shop for souvenirs and oddments, and don't miss the fine aquarium (closed Tuesdays). The Pier is open daily; individual shop and restaurants hours may vary. It's at 800 Second Avenue N.E. 813-821-6164.

SeaCentre is the redevelopment of a fourteen-block stretch of **Jacksonville Beach** that was a grand boardwalk during the 1930s. 904-798-9148.

Index

Other titles in the *Under Sail* series:
California Under Sail ($9.95)
New England Under Sail ($12.95)
Florida Under Sail ($9.95)

Spring 1995
New York–New Jersey Under Sail ($9.95)

Available at bookstores or order directly from the publisher
(add $3.00 shipping and handling for direct orders):

Country Roads Press
P.O. Box 286
Castine, Maine 04421
Toll-free phone number: **800-729-9179**